W9-CPM-229

THE
Day Is Gone

By

Alyse Gregory

NEW YORK

E. P. Dutton & Company, Inc.

1948

Copyright 1948, by E. P. Dutton & Co., Inc.
All rights reserved. Printed in the U.S.A.

FIRST EDITION

¶ *No part of this book may be reproduced in any form without permission in writing from the publisher, except by a reviewer who wishes to quote brief passages in connection with a review written for inclusion in magazine or newspaper or radio broadcast.*

To

AGNES DE LIMA

The day is gone, and all its sweets are gone.

JOHN KEATS

To a man of sense a few intelligent people constitute a more alarming audience than a crowd of fools.

PLATO's Symposium

CONTENTS

Contents

PREFACE

WHEN I set myself the task of writing my life my desire was to reveal with candor and simplicity the most intimate secrets of my heart and the most significant events of my days. I found that my memory was so faulty, and my mind so indolent and so refractory, and my discretion so cunningly persuasive that I was being continually thwarted in this all too innocent endeavor. The words my pen traced were but a pale reflection of the confusions and follies that have run through my hours. This is a manner of failure that most scrupulous writers share, life and art being two quite different things. Life is forever in flight, art forever in pursuit. Art requires order, detachment, and perpetual alertness whereas our minds are constitutionally incoherent and trained in self-deception. Everything conspires to make us superficial, to separate us from what is disturbing to our pride, to "gloss our self-delusion with a muddled thought." I would have liked to view my life as a whole with a serene and lucid wisdom, but my days did not lend themselves to such lofty contemplation. I have sought experience with no purpose except that of awareness and truth with no direction except that of an obscure and urgent desire to understand at all costs. My life has been no steady progression from darkness to light. It has been full of inconsistencies, the thread snapped, the story taken up elsewhere; it has been lived on different levels inaccessible one to the other.

This cannot fail but give formlessness to my narrative. I am not what I was and what I was lies under so many buried selves that to resurrect each in turn is too heavy a tax on my imaginative powers. As to dates and a proper sequence of events my memory is, like that of Montaigne, – "marvelously treacherous." It would have seemed rash under the circumstances to attempt to write of my life at all. This thought occurred to me, I fear, too late, and I have consoled myself by meditating that all lives, whatever they may be, and however imperfectly revealed, are unique, and for this reason of interest to others. In a few instances, where I have deemed it expedient, I have altered the names of persons and places.

Chydyok,
Chaldon Herring,
Dorchester,
Dorset.

THE DAY IS GONE

Chapter I

CHILDHOOD

THE earliest memory of my childhood has to do with some sugared peppermints kept in a Dresden china bonbon dish that stood on the table of our parlor. I had been forbidden by my mother to touch them and I struggled hard to obey her, but I could never enter the room that my attention did not at once fasten upon this inviting dish with its pretty pattern of flowers. Finally temptation became too strong and one day I tremblingly removed the cover and snatching some in my hand fled guiltily out of the door. No sooner had the delicious flavor gone from my palate than a feeling of uneasiness began to replace my short-lived pleasure. I wondered whether I should confess what I had done to my mother, but lacked the necessary courage. At last I struck upon a compromise. I would go to her and beg her "just for once" to let me have some of the peppermints, and if she consented I would refrain from taking them, wiping out my misdeed by this abstention. My mother was sitting with some sewing in a room known to us as the Little Green Room. I put my arms around her neck, and giving her a cajoling kiss, made my casuistical demand.

"But," she said, "you have just had some."

"Oh, no," I denied.

"I know you have from your breath." It was decided that as a punishment I should be put to bed an hour earlier than usual.

Wide awake and in disgrace, I was abandoned to my unhappy thoughts. I would hear the footsteps of cheerful people moving unconcernedly about the house and a disastrous loneliness, mingled with a confused sense of injury and injustice, settled upon me. It was the first time that in any important matter I had found my mother's heart closed to me. I longed to be forgiven and consoled, as well as commended for my good intentions. This incident left a deep impression on my mind. It caused me in some obscure manner to distrust the world about me.

I used to sleep in a child's cot at the head of which was a small window, a window of magic and terror. I would think I saw figures floating through it – dwarfs with long white beards, witches with their broomsticks, bent figures with malevolent, jeering faces that would dance round my bed mocking me. I would bury my head under the bedclothes and remain rigid for long periods, waiting for them to go. On one occasion I brought the whole household to me by my cries, but I could make no one understand and felt more than ever frightened and alone.

At the age of four I was taken by my father in his buggy to a kindergarten. He was to return for me at the end of the morning. I was given a little chair at a desk, and the teacher, with an ingratiating smile, spilled a box of jackstraws in front of me. I viewed these mysterious, fiddling objects with a sensation of helpless alarm. They seemed to open out before me hours of painful tedium to be crowned at the end by certain failure.

I glanced covertly around at the other children, all so obediently engrossed, and I had but one desire, to escape forever from this place. The children were allowed to absent themselves to go to the privy, and presently I raised my hand and received a nod from the teacher.

No sooner was I in the hall than I got my hat and coat, and creeping on tiptoe out of the door, began running in a direction from where I could not be seen. I came finally to a copse where two men were sawing down a tree.

"Well, little girl, how did you get here?" one of them said. Then the other man remarked in a hearty tone: "Well, if this ain't Dr. Gregory's little girl!"

Everyone in Norfield knew my father. Without questioning me further, he set out with me in the direction of my home.

My mother, when I was led in, first looked astonished and then laughed as if the occasion were one for merriment. She never scolded me and she never made me return to the kindergarten. It would have undoubtedly been better for my character had she done so, but she had herself made an art of avoiding what was disagreeable in life, and she wished to smooth the path for others as well.

We children all adored our mother. She was very pretty, with dark, vivacious eyes, a charming smile, and a sprightly intelligence. Her grandfather had founded a university in the Middle West. One of her uncles was a well-known scholar and had published a book on the philosophy of Spinoza. Her father had owned a fashionable boys' school and was the author of textbooks used in schools throughout the country. He lived with us until his death, a mild, studious old man who wore large, steel-rimmed spectacles through which he peered with a gentle abstraction, while he moved as silently up and down the stairs as a shadow.

His favorite pastime was reading through the encyclopedia,

a pleasure his granddaughter has come to appreciate in her latter years; for from the ape to the zoetrope is a wide loop of an intricately interwoven web, and to pursue knowledge is the best way of avoiding falling into traps.

My mother had been a gifted child and a rebel, having shocked her parents while still in short frocks by announcing that she did not believe in the Bible. She had a touch of the artist and liked out-of-the-way characters. She was a good mother and an exciting one. She made and mended our dresses, and she taught us to be considerate of others. She was gay and loving, and yet as a child I remember, side by side with my dependent adoration of her, a sense of frustration, of being thrust back, misunderstood. The two words that perpetually pursued me were "intense" and "sensitive." "You're too intense, you mustn't take things so hard;" or, "You're too sensitive." These words I came to hate so bitterly that I determined no one should ever again be able to tell me I was sensitive, and I used to try more and more cunningly to hide my feelings.

As a very little girl, just after I had learned to write, I was once deeply grieved by something my mother had said to me and came to the conclusion that I would run away. I got a sheet of paper and wrote on it: "Your words have cutted me like a knife. I am leaving your roof forever." I placed it on my mother's dressing table and was about to go down the stairs when I heard her come in at the front door. I drew back and got into a large clothes hamper that was kept in the hall. Finally my mother came up the stairs, followed by my father, and I heard her read aloud the words to him, and then I heard her laugh. This laugh lodged deep in my heart, and I never forgot it, though anyone in her place could hardly have failed to laugh.

My father, who was a doctor, was a man of middle stature with a noble brow, expressive gray eyes, a Roman nose, and drooping mustaches. His kindness was secret and far-reaching. He remained all his life liberal with servants, smuggling them extra sums of money, sending them to entertainments at the most inopportune moments, and treating them with more indulgence than he was apt to show towards himself. The people that could be most certain of receiving prompt consideration from my father were tramps, beggars, Negroes, the very poor, and traveling salesmen – from whom he always bought something. This was a fact so well known that he was continually being visited by tramps, one having passed on the "tip" to the other.

My father was baffled by my mother. Her social poise, her ready wit, her sensitive nerves, her glancing charm, her levity all combined to bewilder and undermine him. My mother was estranged by my father's habit of complaining. She herself never complained. She hid her fears, her disappointments, and her illnesses. She considered a loss of control among the worst disgraces. My father was, under everything, benevolent to the point of folly, a simple-complicated man, descended from the oldest American stock, brought up in the rigors of a New England homestead, with a love of flowers, animals, and all homely things, yet with a natural melancholy and a habit of self-depreciation and discontent that made others victims of his changing humors.

My mother had a belief, always staunchly held, that everyone should be allowed to live his own life, and she encouraged our amusements and welcomed our friends. She loved pretty clothes, and it used to be a continual trouble to me as a child that I was always being dressed up. Her dependence upon my father for money made her secretive, and she had no outlet for her unusual gifts. My father and my brother gave playful encouragement to what they least respected in her. I decided, when I was old enough to make judgments, that men preferred women "tricky."

Among the things that left a strong impression on me during my earliest years was a large frosted globe, lighted with a carbon burner that, like a gigantic pendent moonstone, hung directly in front of our house. Every morning a man would arrive and, lowering it by a pulley, put in a new burner, removing as he did so the dead moths. There were moths of every variety, some almost as large as humming birds, and others as small as the petals of a veronica. These dazzling insects that had met their death in so dire a fashion would haunt my imagination.

In the spring I went with other little girls to search for wild flowers – a pleasure long anticipated – trailing arbutus with tough stalk and deliciously scented blossom, purple hepatica with hairy stem, wild anemone, almost too tender to pluck, Dutchman's breeches, exciting for its name, and white violets hiding in the grass.

In the summer my sister and I took turns visiting some cousins who lived far out in the country where my father had been born. We used to paddle about in a boat on a pond with pond lilies growing in it, flowers that entranced me. I could not understand how anything so fairy-like could come up out of muddy water. I was daring, physically, and could win races, take flying leaps from haylofts, and climb far out onto the swaying branches of the apple trees. From my bedroom window I could see the large yellow moon in the summer sky, with the air stirring the curtains, and the night seeming different from the nights in my own home – more hollow, more mysterious. Sometimes the hoot of an owl would make my flesh creep. My cousin Bessie, a matter-of-fact little girl, slept in the same room with me, and it used to be reassuring to know that she was there.

The time at last came for me to enter a school. The only one within easy reach of our home was a public school. The pupils were boisterous and rude-mannered. Among them were two little colored children – brother and sister. They used to fascinate me, their voices were so musical, their manners so gentle. They appeared always in freshly starched linen, their shoes shining like their faces. They never answered back when they were mocked, but clung tightly to each other's hand, the little girl's woolly plaits standing out from her head, the little boy's eyes sober and puzzled.

My father had a liking for the Negroes and took care of the poor among them without charging them fees. He contributed money to their churches, and the colored ministers, scraping low in glossy silk hats, ingratiating and consequential, came frequently to solicit his help. He sometimes attended their churches, the only white man present. He did this in no spirit of condescension.

At our school was a little English boy called Johnnie Whittaker, who brought me strawberry shrubs, which, when pressed in the palm of the hand, gave out a delicious scent. He wore a broad white collar and a little brown velvet jacket and did not speak like the other children. To this day I associate this wine-red fragrant flower with the name of this charming little boy.

My parents soon took me away from this school and sent me with my sister to a private one, a two-mile walk from our home. My sister seemed to learn her lessons with the utmost ease. I would look at her with envy. It was not that I was dull or slow-witted, but the moment I thought something was expected of me a film would come over my mind, and my shame at failing would add to my general sense of calamity. My sister sometimes helped me with my lessons at home, just as a strong swimmer will, with a casual pull, take a weak swmimer into shore when he sees him getting short of breath. My sister had a fiery temper which she combined with an unusually sweet disposition. The color would mount to her cheeks, her eyes would flash, and the other children would run away intimidated. In a second, like flame blown across the surface of a still lake, the anger would have vanished. She was very pretty, a brunette with brown eyes, a slim figure, and an oval face.

The most dominant influence in my life was that of my brother. He obsessed my thoughts. He was four years my senior, a gifted, lively boy, petted by everyone, particularly my mother, precocious in his lessons, and proficient at sports. He was probably no greater tease than are most brothers, but he certainly excelled in thinking up new and ingenious ways of confounding me. I was afraid of him, envious of him, and there was sown in my mind a seed of rebellion against tyranny and the ignominies of a girl's life that has borne fruit to this day.

Every Saturday, during the winter months, I attended, with my brother and sister, a dancing class. Our Irish coachman, Charles Caffrey, took us to our lessons, sometimes in a sleigh over the frozen snow to the sound of jingling bells. Our teacher, known as Professor Newell, wore a full dress suit, and his slippers were as pointed as a stiletto. He had the haughty bearing of an impresario. As soon as we were lined up and the first chords of the piano had sounded he would call out orders like the rat-a-tat-tat of a drumbeat. I took to dancing as a bird to wings. He taught my sister and me a Spanish *seguidilla*, which we performed with other show pupils in the theatres of adjacent towns. We wore short apple-green accordion-pleated skirts, black velvet bolero jackets, and had each a pair of castanets that we struck with fiery abandon to the intoxicating rhythm of the music.

Chapter II

DISGRACE AND ILLUMINATION

When I was twelve years old, my parents moved into a large house near the center of the town, which was thought more convenient for my father's growing practice. All through my childhood I was familiar with the sound of the telephone ringing in the middle of the night, and of my father going down the stairs and out into the stable to have his horse harnessed. He would often have to drive far into the country. Once some men tried to hold him up on a lonely strip of road, known as Devil's Gap. They rushed out from behind some trees and grasped the horse's bridle. My father swung his whip, the horse plunged forward, and they fell away firing two shots. This incident haunted my imagination for many years afterward, and even when I was fully grown I could never pass through this particular locality without experiencing a vague shiver of alarm.

My father had some lively horses. One, called Bob, a great bay, had a tail as strong as a truncheon. If, through lack of vigilance, he was allowed to get it well-fastened over the rein, disaster was imminent. Even the gentlest twitch, the most propitiatory drawing in of the rein would send him bolting down the road, his eyeballs bloodshot, his nostrils spouting froth, and his hoofs pounding like the charge of a Cossack brigade. One had to wait until whim or necessity impelled him to raise his tail of his own volition. These were breathless moments, especially as he was so skittish that the mere sight of a woman's bonnet could make him caper and rear.

Another horse, Rupee, was jet black, with a long, flowing mane and dainty hoofs that made a noise like the shaking of dice in a metal box as he rattled over the turnpike. He followed his own categorical imperative, being as impervious to the tug of a rein as a cat to persuasion when stalking a bird. He advanced by some mysterious law of his own.

My favorite horse was Daisy. She had a brown coat and a white star on her forehead. She had only one bad fault. She was apt to run away at the sight of a tramcar. These cars had replaced the old horse-drawn cars while I was still a child. They passed infrequently through the town and outlying districts, but there was always a chance that one of them might loom suddenly into view.

My father took me frequently on his rounds with him, and I used to study the heels, tail, and disposition of each horse with apprehensive absorption. There was always a moment of suspense when he drew up in front of a patient's house as to whether he would hitch the horse or I should be given the reins to hold. I was too proud or too tongue-tied to offer a plea, but would wait, like a prisoner in the dock, for the verdict. My father seemed entirely free from such poor-spirited preoccupations, although he was continually being run away with. Once I saw him creep on hands and knees from under his upturned carriage. By some miracle neither he nor his coachman was ever seriously injured, although they had some narrow escapes.

Sometimes my sister and I used to be driven to a great house in the center of a large property near the seashore to play with two little girls called Woodberry. We would be dressed in our best flowered silks – my sister in pink and I in blue – and the occasion would be one of grave responsibility. Mr. Woodberry was an impressive-looking man who moved in and out among his costly possessions with an air of languid and melancholy patronage. His wife greeted us when we came and bade us good-by when we left. Otherwise no word ever seemed to pass her lips. A stately footman in livery laid a table where we had cups of sweet chocolate with whipped cream, and cakes with pistachio filling. The little girls spoke in thin, stilted voices and seemed more like marionettes than real flesh and blood. It was a relief when our father came to fetch us away.

After we had settled in our new home, an old friend of my mother's family, Nathaniel Trowbridge, came continually to visit us. He lived in the adjoining town, in a large house, by himself. He was the head of a publishing firm in New York and traveled daily to his business. We children called him Uncle Nat and came to think of him as a true uncle. He was a tall man with an upright carriage and a drooping mustache and had a reputation for being witty. He would drive up to our door in a shining trap direct from the train, and my sister or I would hasten out to him. More often it would be I, as my sister spent most of her spare moments preparing her lessons.

I would climb up to my uncle Nat's side, and he would flourish his whip, which was the signal for the horses, fresh from the stable, to be off. They were thoroughbred horses with glossy sorrel coats and long, arching necks. One was called Sport and the other Steady. We would dash through the town, up Mill Hill, past the old borough hall, and gallop full pace over the road towards a seaside resort where drinks were served. My uncle would rein in at the door of this establishment, and a waiter in a spotless white apron would come hurrying out to us. My uncle usually ordered gin and bitters, and I hesitated between a ginger ale and a sarsaparilla.

In the evenings, Uncle Nat would bring his violin with him to our house, and my mother would accompany him on the piano. My mother was musical and had played the piano at public performances as a child. She also had a charming singing voice, with notes as pure as those of the English blackbird. Uncle Nat, besides using his bow with a vigor more befitting a hewer of trees than a musician, played continually out of tune. A look of desperation would show for a moment in my mother's eyes as he opened his violin case and pulled from his pocket a white silk handkerchief with which to dust his instrument before settling it under his determined chin.

In the summer, Uncle Nat took a cottage on the sound, and I used to go there to visit him. My greatest happiness was to run out in the very early morning at low tide and watch the fishermen, their trousers rolled up over their thighs, netting for soft clams. The oozy mud would be one vast spectacle of scurrying hermit crabs, and the sandy beach would be strewn thick with mussel shells.

When we came to live in our new home, my sister and I changed our school for another private one for girls. It was near the top of a steep hill, which in winter was frequently frozen over with a thick coating of ice. Charles, my father's coachman, sometimes would be ordered to drive us there, and the horse's hoofs could not grip the ice. When, after prodigious strainings and frequent false starts, the gate came at last into view, we might even then begin sliding back down the whole incline, the horse's hindquarters pressed tight against the dashboard, hardly an inch from my shaking knees. After school we would spin down the hill on our geography books, a feat at which I was especially expert, more expert than I was at my lessons. My lessons were, indeed, one long series of humiliations and despairs. I used to think that if I could outgrow the necessity for taking examinations, no word of complaint would ever again pass my lips. I would watch my sister conquering every fresh task as easily as a toad hops, or a dog laps up water; whereas I could not do even a simple sum in arithmetic without getting the wrong answer.

The dreaded moment for our half-yearly examinations had at last come round. By some stroke of fortune I managed to get through my history and English papers, but when the mathematics test was placed in front of me, the figures on the great double sheets of foolscap seemed to freeze my thoughts altogether. Just as I had, on my first kindergarten day, risked all to escape, I now decided to do the same.

Slipping through the door and out of the house, I stepped onto a narrow dirt road, and seeing a coal cart going leisurely along in front of me, hastened to overtake it. The driver, half drowsing, was holding the reins loosely, and I jumped lightly up on the back of the wagon. It was the season of the year when "the apple blossoms flew white for Spring." Everywhere fresh green leaves were showing and the notes of phoebes sounded in the dazzling sunshine. A feeling of utter happiness took possession of me. I did not care whether disgrace awaited me, or what my future was to hold. I had never before felt such a surge of exaltation in all my bones. "Let me be true to this moment," I thought. "Let me never forget this moment."

By going through various back streets, I could reach the Norfield River. Only the poorest houses, often mere shacks, were scattered along its banks, occupied for the most part by Negroes and Italians. I loved to watch the wild birds wheeling, soaring, dipping; the ships moving silently through the water; the sunset reflected on brimming tide or on mud banks dotted with multitudinous, minute, glittering pools. On Saturday afternoons I often went to a grassy spot near a little white house, set in a grove of spruce trees at the water's edge. One day I saw an old man dragging in a fishing boat with a long rope. He had a white beard and wore spectacles. He told me his name was Captain Jennings and asked me whether I would like to go out in his boat with him. I accepted with delight. I did not tell anyone about this adventure, but at every opportunity I returned to this old man, who taught me to row and to feather my oars in the most accomplished manner.

Chapter III

ARRIVAL IN PARIS

WHEN I was in my fifteenth year, a niece of Uncle Nat's came to visit him. Her name was Nina Chad. She was a painter, whose home was in Paris, and she bewitched us all. I was supposed to have musical talent, and when she heard me sing she invited me to go to Paris to stay with her and her husband to pursue my musical education. She was leaving in a fortnight's time, and it was decided that I should follow, under the patronage of some acquaintances of hers.

I sailed on the *St. Louis* in the late autumn. For hours I would stand gazing out at the sea "with all its stormy crests that smoke against the sky." At night I would watch the bow of the ship cleaving the dark waters, dividing them into two cataracts of swirling, seething foam that grew thinner and thinner until it disappeared, like white feathers, on the trough of the swell. The captain noticed that I went to places forbidden to passengers, but the sailors were friendly, and except during a bad storm I was left alone. It was my first imaginative revelation of the ocean's immemorial flood.

There was a soldierly-looking German on board the ship, with a long scar down one cheek which, it was whispered, he had received in a duel. I would sometimes hear him playing the piano in the dining saloon and would go in to listen. He discovered that I was on my way to Paris to study singing and made me fetch some songs. In the end he accompanied me at the concert given for the benefit of seamen's charities. In the middle of my song he slid off the piano stool and landed in a ridiculous posture at the knees of an elderly spinster lady, which appeared to cause the audience more pleasure than anything on the program. With a look of abashed dignity he picked himself up, and we began the song over again, but I was so nervous, and the ship rolled in so disconcerting a manner that my first appearance as a singer in public could hardly be called a success.

Paris, as I was driven through the streets in a rattling fiacre, on a chill, foggy morning, seemed not at all as I had pictured it. The buildings were as gray as the sky. The Chads' studio was in Neuilly. It was a vast room with a platform for a model and a large, round stove that gave out a delicious warmth. My bedroom was up a tiny spiral staircase and was just large enough for a bed and wardrobe. Edgar Chad was a tall man with a black beard and friendly eyes. I was homesick that first night and anxious when I thought of all the money my father had spent on me. I hoped I would disappoint no one.

There was a girls' school just around the corner from the Chads' studio, and arrangements had been made for me to take solfège lessons from a teacher there. I was to begin my singing lessons at once.

My teacher, who lived on the Rue Joubert, had been a famous opera star. Her name was Marie Rôze. She was now old and stout, but retained lingering charm. She wore a purple ribbon to show that she had been a Dreyfusard. She had a parrot that used to ape her pupils. It would sing arpeggios and scales and fragments of operas, stopping to squawk out: "*Non, non, pas bien, il faut recommencer.*" It would intersperse its performance with shrieks of maniacal laughter. It was a most surprising bird and she adored it.

I took three lessons a week and was soon learning roles from operas – Lakmé, Marguerite, Manon. My tramcar came to a halt at the Madeleine, where I changed to a bus, and I would stop to look at the flower women, their ruddy faces showing from behind their stalls of mimosas, chrysanthemums, or daffodils. How much flower women resemble one another the world over, whether in the Piazza di Spagna in Rome, or in Piccadilly in London, or at the Madeleine in Paris – Hogarthian women, vital and ribald!

Though I studied conscientiously, practicing my scales at regular hours, I was otherwise caught up in a whirl of gaiety. Nina Chad was a slender woman with a small oval face and mocking, attractive eyes. She was twenty-six and a born coquette. I was too young seriously to rival her, but I served as an excuse for her to go to balls and parties. Not a week passed that we did not attend some festivity.

The event of the season was the architects' ball. I danced through the whole night with a young Frenchman, though it was more like floating than dancing, for our feet seemed barely to touch the floor. With no man have I ever enjoyed dancing to the same extent, and we parted without even asking one another's names.

It is singular to think of the partners one has danced with in one's youth – this gay debonair procession of young men, many of them now dead, others illiberal, wheezing citizens, with shiny bald heads, offering unheeded advice to a whole new generation of young men, gay and debonair.

Once every month Mme. Rôze gave a musical to show off her pupils. On one of these occasions Massenet was present and accompanied me on the piano when I sang an aria from *Manon.* I did not know until later that this old, white-haired man was Massenet. Mme. Rôze had a friend, M. Rivière, who appeared in tenor roles at the Opéra Comique. We sometimes practiced duets together. He was a plump man who was very proud of his beautiful voice. He would throw back his head and rise on the tips of his toes while the room overflowed like a vessel with his liquid tones.

Early in May an old school friend of Nina's, Rachel Hill, came to Paris, accompanied by two young men who had been representing their university at an international sports tournament. Nina's friend was a striking blonde who had left a compliant husband in Baltimore. She wore provocative frocks and hats tilted at the most fetching angle and was reckless and enterprising. One of the young men, Nick, was her constant attendant, and the other one, Courtney, attached himself to me.

Courtney was twelve years my senior, tall, good-looking, and languid. Not a day passed that we did not meet. He would accompany me to my singing lessons and return for me again. We would drift through the Luxembourg Gardens or visit the Jardin d'Acclamatation or have tea with some acquaintance in the Latin Quarter. Once I rested my hand on the banisters of the stairs and he placed his so that our little fingers touched. A swooning giddiness passed through me, but I discreetly withdrew my hand.

Chapter IV

WITH MME. ROZE IN THE COUNTRY

AT THE beginning of June, Mme. Rôze left Paris for her summer home in the country, and Rachel and I and the two young men went on a bicycling expedition. We would pass through little villages with sloping red-tiled roofs and ancient churches, and with children rattling down cobblestone alleys in wooden clogs, and women kneeling at the sides of rivers washing out their clothes. The nights we spent at wayside inns, Rachel and I usually sharing a room. Our meals we ate at little tables laid out of doors.

Rachel considered me naïve, and I looked at her with envy and some disapproval. She made slight concealment of the fact that she and Nick were lovers. Courtney was more refined than Nick. He came from an old New York family and believed in good form and in treating a girl as he would have his sisters treated. He used to tell me of his home, his family, his future plans in a somewhat drawling tone of voice.

After our return to Paris there was only one week left before the two young men were to sail back to New York. Courtney and I spent most of this week together, meeting for lunch, wandering in the Bois de Boulogne, or taking a boat up the Seine. In the end he kissed me good-by, and I had two wires and a love letter from him before his steamer sailed. I imagined myself in love, yet he had been gone only a short time when my perceptions seemed to spring up, newly born, as if from a long slumber.

With my singing teacher in the country, I had more free time, and Edgar Chad asked me to pose for him. I grew very attached to this good man whose unremitting industry seemed to come from no burning core within him. He might have been a scrupulous compiler of statistics from the manner in which he worked. He had none of that glaze of passion we usually associate with artists.

Every morning I would get up before breakfast and, mounting my bicycle, ride out in the Bois de Boulogne. Suddenly I would see at the far end of the deserted avenue an officer astride a handsome pony, and as we passed each other I would give a swift glance up and meet a pair of bold, dark eyes, immobile and insinuating, and into my marrow would penetrate a delicious, shivering excitement.

It was now the middle of July, and the heat was intense. Mme. Rôze wrote, urging me to stay with her for the rest of the summer at Val Notre Dame, offering to give me a singing lesson daily at a fee no greater than the one I had been paying in Paris. Nina and Edgar decided to close the studio and take a house by the seashore.

Mme. Rôze's house was concealed from the road by a high stone wall, and on fine days we had our meals out in the garden. A young English girl, called Barbara Parsons, was living with us. She was mutely adoring of the aging prima donna. Mme. Rôze had been married to a famous impresario called Mapleton. All this dazzling life seemed to have vanished without leaving any more trace than when the sun has set and the last rosy glow has faded from the sky.

It was difficult to believe, as one looked at this old woman in her plain dresses, that she had been carried on the shoulders of students through cheering crowds, had packed the great opera houses of the world with bedizened women and ogling men, and had been showered with costly trinkets by kings and emperors.

I persuaded her one evening to bring out her jewel box and show us some of her treasures, among them a tiara of diamonds and emeralds. She seemed entirely free of vanity. Indeed she seemed half in a dream much of the time.

M. Rivière arrived usually on a Sunday morning, returning the following evening to Paris. He had a passion for the occult and would get us to sit round a table on which we rested the palms of our hands with our little fingers touching. We would then ask questions, the answers being judged by the way in which the table, an exceptionally talented one, tipped. He always seated himself next to me and would press his thigh gently against mine. We would frequently sing duets together from *La Bohême* or *Manon Lescaut*, and his ringing tones would make the walls of Mme. Rôze's tiny salon shake and vibrate.

Mme. Rôze gave tea parties to her friends, who came from Paris for them. They took place in the garden. Decorous and voluble, the guests would beck and nod at one another like cormorants on sea ledges, observing the punctilios of courteous intercourse without too strict a care for the meaning of words.

Once Barbara's father, Mr. Parsons, came to spend two nights, with us. He was a pompous, pot-bellied little man with a complacent self-absorption. Mme. Rôze gave a luncheon party in his honor, and during the fish course he had a choking fit. It began with a few agitated coughs and gradually became a series of prolonged gasps. Everyone sat frozen in silence. Not a fork was raised during these suspended moments; and what struck me most forcibly, giving me a new, startling vision of life, was the fact that no one looked concerned. No one rushed to pat him on the back or to fill his glass with water or to call a doctor, yet everyone expected that he might at any moment die in his chair.

I have often recalled that table of mummified figures, their eyes set in a glare of cautious fear, while the interminable gasps of Mr. Parsons were pushed out and drawn in, drawn in and pushed out, and the fish got colder and colder on the platter. When the tension was at last relaxed, and, with the tears streaming down his round, bloated countenance, he grasped again with indomitable, pudgy fingers his knife and fork, no one congratulated him on his miraculous escape from death. The incident was treated, rather, as an awkward *faux pas* to be politely ignored.

Of those weeks at Val Notre Dame perhaps what I remember most clearly is the look of the cornflowers holding up their sky-blue heads in the yellow rye, and the fields of blood-red poppies, and the songs of the nightingales that would come through my window as I lay unable to sleep. It would seem at times as if the whole universe were a crystal bell ringing with their melody.

After leaving Mme. Rôze, I spent two months perfecting my French at Mme. Monourys' school in Neuilly. At meal times I sat beside two German sisters whose appetite used to cause me a secret uneasiness, since they were served just before me. Even a platter fresh in from the kitchen, heaped high with food, could, after they had helped themselves, be left without enough on it to throw to a hungry chaffinch on a frosty morning. Eating in mixed company has always seemed to me one of the forms of discomfort to which human beings have unwisely subjected themselves. I have always shunned the eye of a dog when he is waiting for scraps to be thrown him, and the human eye has something of the same expression.

I made friends with a Russian girl, Varvara. We used to go for walks together. She would tell me of her home, her brothers and sisters and her life would seem to me full of poetry and romance. She was studying painting, and everything that she did and said was touched with a kind of reckless ardor. We continued to correspond for many years after we had both left Paris.

In November my mother wrote saying that my father wanted me to come home. I said good-by to my Paris life with regret mingled with excitement and apprehension, not knowing what the future was to hold.

My brother was taking a course in a medical college in New York, and it was decided that I should stay with him and continue my singing lessons. We rented a small flat on a rather sordid uptown street. He was attending classes and lectures most of the time, and I was left to my own resources.

The singing teacher to whom I went was a German woman named Fräulein Hauser. She was large-boned and plain, with thin, graying, snuff-colored hair parted in the middle with the precision of a yard rule. Wisps were continually getting into her eyes, and she would push them out with her great knuckles, a look of goaded frustration on her face. She was supposed to have been a famous coloratura star and to have lost her singing voice after an illness. She had certainly never got it back, but she was a thorough musician and taught me, in German, songs of Schubert, Schumann, and Brahms, and the role of Susanna in *The Marriage of Figaro*. I was supposed to have three lessons a week, but she offered to give me a lesson daily without extra charge.

She had a friend, Professor Ernst, a professional pianist, who arrived every afternoon at the hour when I finished my lesson. She would invite me to stay for coffee and would serve thick slices of black bread with fresh butter. After we had had our coffee, Professor Ernst would go to the piano. His touch could be as light as the falling of a rose petal on moss, of a dove's feather on snow. He knew whole scores by heart. It was usually to Beethoven or Schumann he returned, or to Wagner, who was in fashion in those days. Then suddenly he would lift up his hands, wheel round, rise, and make a low bow. He was shy and reserved.

In the spring of this year my brother entered a hospital as an intern. We gave up the flat, and I arranged to come to New York twice a week for my singing lessons.

My father had been attending a visiting concert singer in our town, and when he told her he had a daughter who had studied singing in Paris, she asked to hear my voice.

She was a vital woman, with a large bosom, piercing black eyes, and coarse, crimped hair. She praised my voice extravagantly but condemned the method by which I was being taught. When she saw my father she told him that she would like to take me to live with her and prepare me at her own expense to sing in opera, a prospect that filled me with dismay. I was persuaded, however, to give up my lessons with Fräulein Hauser.

I did not take this decision lightly, nor did Fräulein Hauser, who offered me a written agreement that she would refund half of all I had paid to her if she did not within six months' time obtain for me a role in light opera.

I always retained an affection for this old woman with her big bones, her homely ways, her simplicity and sobriety and large Teutonic hospitality. She gave me a love for the songs of Schubert and Schumann that remains with me to this day, and I felt more deeply inspired by the spirit of the music I was seeking to interpret under her training than with any other teacher.

Chapter V

NEAPOLITAN DELIGHTS

MY SISTER was now married and living with her husband in Naples, where he was American consul. They invited me to visit them, and I sailed from New York in the early summer. There was a famous astronomer on board the ship, much older than I, who used to follow me about holding a copy of *Le Lys Rouge* under his arm. He was thin, stooping, and pale, with a protruding forehead and a tapering chin. He had intelligent eyes that regarded me with a sly and lively curiosity. His conversation was remote from the heavenly spheres, and I learned a great deal from him, not from what he said, but from the reflections he stirred up in my mind. When he asserted that the sole thing men asked for in women was *joie de vivre*, it aroused my secret indignation. It was certainly not Baudelaire's standard of feminine charm when he wrote:

Que m'importe que tu sois sage?
Sois belle et sois triste! Les pleurs
Ajoutent un charme au visage,
Comme le fleuve au paysage;
L'orage rajeunit les fleurs.

What men wanted women to be, apparently, was an image of their own making.

My sister and brother-in-law were living on the ground floor of a large villa at the foot of a long, winding lane on the edge of the Bay of Naples. An Italian duchess inhabited the floor above. I had never seen a person of title before and awaited my first glimpse of her with curiosity.

Her equipage, drawn by a pair of prancing horses, would await her at the top of the lane, with a man in livery to drive and another to assist her to her seat. Immaculate and regal, they seemed more to resemble what I had looked for in the aristocracy than the bedizened lady they were conveying.

Wherever my brother-in-law, Homer, was, good times were sure to prevail. His geniality was proverbial. He was a member of a rowing club and belonged to the Neapolitan tennis club, and the English one as well. My sister was by temperament a scholar and a poet, and a life of social gaieties was not native to her. She entertained continually, however. Everyone in Neapolitan society had an afternoon at home, and life was one round of calling, dancing, bathing, sailing, and playing tennis; and I, being young and vivacious, was soon surrounded by cavaliers – tall, short, plump, and lean, with monocles, with beards with mustaches, and without them.

I used to sing at my sister's "at homes" a song beginning with the verse:

> I know a maiden fair to see,
> Take care, take care.
> She can both false and faithful be,
> Beware, beware.
> Trust her not, she is fooling thee,
> She is fooling thee.

There was an old General, erect and braided, who, whenever he saw me, would at once cock his head to one side like a rapt Chanticleer, and, wagging an index finger, mischievously repeat the words "Bee-ware, bee-ware," Several young men learned this song by heart.

I made friends with a Spanish woman, known by the name of Belita. She had black slanting eyes and a mocking smile. She used to invite me to drive in the mornings through the Via Chiaja to one of the cafés where fashionable society gathered for a glass of vermouth before their midday meal. We went on several bathing expeditions, accompanied by officers with clinking swords. One Captain held his head well out of the water so that not a drop could wet his handsome mustache.

Once I spent a night with Belita in her villa. I was surprised to see her in the morning wearing a black satin nightgown trimmed with little rosettes of pink gauze. Her husband, an Englishman, was engaged in some business that took him out of the city for days at a time. She always referred to him as if he were the darling of her hours: "Dear Ferdie, he is the sweetest man in the world. I wouldn't do a *thing* to trouble him." She managed her intrigues so as to save him all uneasiness. He was, indeed, that rarest of all curiosities, an entirely contented husband.

I soon received two proposals of marriage, one from a young cavalry lieutenant with large, sad eyes and a fair mustache, and one from a captain of the Bersagliere, who presented me with a handsome Bersagliere plume.

How could I help but like Italians? They were all so charming to me, and I have never deviated from my admiration for these gracious people, so alive to the pleasures of the moment, so essentially civilized. I have never known an Italian to forget his good manners. I am sure that were he about to stab you he would do it with a gallant compliment. When the Baron d'Holbach visited England he referred to the inhabitants of this invincible island as "people on whose countenance you never see confidence, friendship, gaiety, sociability, but on every face, " 'What is there in common between you and me?' " It is just these things that the Italian, even more than the Frenchman, reveals on his countenance – confidence, friendship, gaiety, sociability.

One day my steamer friend, Dr. Meikeljohn, asked me to go to Capri with him. He seemed a little slow after my Italian acquaintances. He wore a green felt hat and carried an umbrella in blazing sunshine. "I fear," he said, "I lack *brio*."

I soon made a new friend who caused me to lose interest in Belita. She was living in a villa with her two little children, Clive and Betty, aged five and seven. She was married to a well-known writer who had remained in New Mexico, bidding fair to do so for the rest of his days.

I often wondered how Mrs. X . . . . . managed to take in so much, when, like M. Guizot, she was so skilled in eliminating all sights and sounds about her. I think inveterate talkers make up for their lack of attention by the retentiveness of their memories. If one can once drive a remark home, it remains stuck like an arrow in a target, and in the course of years many such arrows must have come to a resting place.

She was a large, heavily built woman, and she pushed forward in pursuit of adventure as an elephant pushes through a jungle. She meant to get to the true heart of life, to study historic monuments and move among great ideas. When she asked me to accompany her on a walking expedition, I accepted at once.

Sorrento was our starting point, and it was decided to send the children ahead in a carriage to await us at the villages where we were to spend the nights.

The sun beat down upon the glittering sea and upon the dazzling roads that burnt the balls of my feet through the thin soles of my sandals. Nothing stemmed the flow of Mrs. X . . . . .'s conversation, which alternated between large generalizations and unfavorable comments on the character of her famous mother-in-law, an astonishing old woman, as full, apparently, of spleen as a cuttlefish of ink.

The children would be anxiously awaiting us at some little inn. We would have our meal in the garden while the lovely southern twilight descended about us, and I could relax my limbs at ease.

On one occasion we visited an ancient Cistercian monastery where we were shown round by a young priest with an emaciated countenance and furtive eyes. To my amazement I saw Mrs. X . . . . . turn suddenly upon him, a torrent of conversation in her native tongue pouring from her lips, with an occasional *bestia,* and *cattivo* thrown in as a sure clue to her intention.

It seems that he had pinched her thigh and this had aroused her to an indignant attack upon the whole edifice of his ancient and poetic faith. The poor young man looked sick with mortification and frustration, and I felt most sorry for him.

Pompeii was our last objective, and we arrived there just at dark. As soon as we had finished our supper, Mrs. X . . . . . went upstairs with the children, and I stole down the path and out of the gate.

The ruins were only a short distance away. By leaving the

road and mounting onto a bank through some nettles, I could see the whole little town – its streets, its roofless shops and houses, its crumbling temple pillars. Nothing broke the stillness. I was alone in the moon-enchanted summer night.

I did not tell Mrs. X....., when we visited the ruins on the following morning, of my solitary pilgrimage. Our most exquisite experiences are often dim to ourselves, and in seeking to reveal them, we lose them altogether.

That same afternoon I said good-by to my friends. They were returning to Sorrento, and I was to drive to Castellammare and from there to take a boat to Naples.

My coachman was a casual-looking fellow with a flower stuck behind his ear and a round straw hat poised nonchalantly on the back of his head. To be away from Mrs. X..... was like coming out of range of a mountain torrent. My senses felt volatile, airy. Everything I saw excited me – the little boys, wearing brightly colored caps, astride diminutive mules; the women in their laced bodices and full skirts balancing earthenware pitchers on their heads; huge cactus plants casting black shadows on dazzling walls, above which rose the cool, shining leaves of orange trees.

Presently it was borne in upon me that the carriage in which I was so happily seated was swaying in an unusual manner. "*Non cosí presto.*" I called to the driver. He pulled at the horse's bit, but the beast continued to plunge down the precipitous incline at headlong gallop. On one side was a sheer rise of rock, and on the other, a wall with the sea far below.

As we came to a sharp bend in the road, I placed my foot on the step of the carriage and jumped to the ground – as I had done from rapidly moving buses. A second later the carriage had been overturned, and the horse, breaking his harness, went thundering on down the mountainside and was lost to view.

The coachman crawled out from under the wreckage, emitting a volley of native oaths. In less time than it takes to spin a coin, three carriages had dashed up, each soliciting my patronage. I finished my trip behind a lean, gray horse more inclined to come to a halt than to run away, driven by an old man who appeared to be sound asleep.

Chapter VI

FAREWELL TO PLEASURE

A SUCCESSION of diversions continued to fill my hours: expeditions by moonlight to little seaside restaurants; visits to officers' barracks, where I was presented with martial poems and military mementos by graceful young lieutenants who flashed me ambiguous glances; and always as a background to this life of pleasure, the changing beauties of the bay. At night I would hear the waves lapping up on the shore, and snatches of melody would drift in through the open window.

From my earliest childhood I had been subject to abrupt transitions of mood. At the very height of my gaiety I would be suddenly transfixed with an awareness of the insubstantiality of everything about me, and people would seem like apparitions floating in a mirage. I never told anyone of these sensations, and they would gradually go.

What I loved best was to watch the fishermen pulling in their catches of glistening silver fish in great nets under the scorching rays of the sun. Many of them were very old men with grizzled hair and little caps on their heads, their shirts laced down the front with fishing tackle.

A funeral procession never failed to astonish me, as, preceded by a brass band blaring out a lugubrious march, it moved through the street, the hearse, draped in a gorgeous velvet pall embossed in gold, flanked by masked and hooded figures.

At that time a large part of the Naples population spent most of its hours on the pavements. Women brushed and combed their sleek locks while they squatted on stools, jesting and quarreling and staring boldly at the passers-by. A flock of sheep would patter along the main thoroughfare, led by a shepherd in a ragged cloak with a tall crook. Carts of oranges and tangerines, glistening like polished golden nuggets, would rattle by; and at certain hours the great procession of Neapolitan society in their shining carriages, drawn by high-stepping horses, with liveried grooms sitting as straight as a barber's pole, would pass down the Chiaja. There would be old ladies, holding tiny parasols over their heads, inclining forward like royalty to acknowledge an obsequious salute, young blades darting glances, expert in intrigue, and aging roués with simpering masks that concealed a hollow despair.

I was sometimes taken to the homes of these members of the Neapolitan noblesse. One little old *Principessa* received us in a palatial salon as dim as a cave, with velvet curtains of a bishop's purple to keep out the light, perhaps to hide the age of her carpets as well as of her countenance, for there were many of the great Italian families that were said to have more crests than soldi.

Only once did I come near to falling in love. Mrs. X..... had on several occasions invited me to meet a young man studying to be a doctor. I was struck by the reserve of his manner. He listened attentively and answered with a hesitating sincerity. This was not the ordinary Neapolitan way of entertaining a young lady; but I was struck even more by his unusual eyes, green as a lion's, that regarded me so intently.

One day he brought his sister with him, a beautiful girl,

who later poisoned herself in a suicide pact with her lover. Suddenly she leaned over and whispered to me in a rapid aside, "Luigi has fallen in love with you." That night I dreamed that Luigi and I met in some mysterious, sinister garden near a fortress from which he had only just escaped. He kissed me on the lips, and I woke with a sensation so delicious and so penetrating that it was as if it had all actually happened.

Mrs. X. . . . ., who had been staying for some weeks in Anacapri, now wrote suggesting that I come to visit her, bringing Luigi with me. The expedition was arranged, and we boarded the little passenger boat in bright sunshine, to the familiar tune of "Santa Lucia."

I thought how foolishly Luigi's sister had misled me, for his conduct could not have been more exemplary. Only now and then the pupils of his eyes would grow large and his hand would tremble. We had our lunch on the terrace of the pension, the children full of shy, eager friendliness, and Mrs. X. . . . . overtopping their voices with fresh and bitter anecdotes about her mother-in-law that she had been storing up for my arrival.

The sun was just beginning to set when she saw Luigi and me off in our carriage, and the landscape was suffused with a rosy glow, the curving shores of Naples shimmering for one suspended moment in the ethereal light. Only the sound of the horse's hoofs as he trotted down the twisting mountain road broke the silence.

A week later I sailed back to America. Luigi sent a farewell letter to the steamer, in which the ardor he had so prudently withheld while opportunity was ripe, now, as I was about to disappear for ever from his native shore, found reckless expression. Love, he wrote, was "*una tortura deliziosa.*"

Chapter VII

NEW HORIZONS

After the novelty of my homecoming had worn off, I was left with a feeling of restlessness. I spent a great deal of time searching out books in our public library. Dostoevsky and Henry James were my two discoveries at this time. I read every volume of each of these authors that the library contained.

With Dostoevsky I lost all sense of my own identity. It was as if I were in a fever, the words burning themselves into my spirit. Nothing could ever be as it was. It was a new universe I had entered, and my own life seemed without depth or significance, yet infinitely extended.

James had a steadying effect and he is perhaps the novelist who, until I began to read Proust, influenced me most strongly. He taught me to seek out drama in the most insignificant daily incident, and that the only really important battles in life are the eternal ones of the ardent and the magnanimous against the cruel and the gross.

I had no one with whom to share these excitements – the most important one being my introduction to poetry. Shelley was the first poet I read. I took a volume of his down from the library shelf and carried it away with me. I had always thought of poetry as something one had to recite at school, highly revered and secretly derided. In these verses I discovered my most intimate self, my moods and fantasies. Walt Whitman was another discovery, and he has always remained a poet to whom I return for inspiration and strength.

For a long time my brother had been coughing badly, and it was discovered that he had consumption. He had become widely known as a surgeon, and people came from all the surrounding towns to consult him. He had a passion for his profession, it had consumed his life. My father, on the other hand, felt a general disbelief in all remedies and all knowledge, and was always proclaiming his ignorance. He could not bear to see his patients suffer and to be unable to cure them, and a combination of self-lacerating pessimism and irrepressible candor made him exhibit his helplessness continually. Yet he had some quality that communicated itself in a sick-room and made him heal people against his own adverse and melancholy judgments. There was nothing professional, no doctor's tricks, but all through my childhood and youth I would, whenever I was ill, feel strength flow back into me at the mere sight of my father's figure at my bedside.

I was too much wrapped up in my own life to realize the seriousness of my brother's illness. What finally brought it home to me was the expression on my mother's face when she heard him cough. She at last persuaded him to give up his practice and go to Saranac Lake, where she soon followed him.

With my mother away, my father was eager to please me and he never complained. He liked bringing in delicacies — muskmelons, peaches, alligator pears, fresh boxes of dates and figs; and my greed for ice cream was never so pampered. Not a day passed that he did not arrive home with a carton of my favorite dessert. All the shopkeepers would pick out their best provisions for him. The servants seemed to have vanished altogether. My mother and brother returned home the last week in October, my brother so restored in health that he soon resumed his practice.

There was visiting in our town another professional singer, who expressed a desire to hear me sing. I rolled up my music in its leather case one morning and went out into the frosty air with the sensation I always experienced when I thought something special was expected of me, a sense of pending disaster combined with an impulse that drove me irresistibly towards the very thing from which I most shrank. As a child it had come to me one day with an unmistakable conviction that I must always take the step forward; I must never draw back from the dangerous, the unknown.

Mrs. Howard was a handsome woman with a commanding carriage. She wore a flowing scarlet crepe de Chine gown that, with her luxuriant black hair and rather glassy eyes, gave her the look of an Eastern priestess. I was reassured by her warm smile. She compared my voice to Melba's and said that it would be "nothing short of a crime" for me not to follow singing as a profession. She was on the point of renting an apartment in New York and asked my father to let me come and live with her as a pupil, paying only the cost of my food. My mother was delighted at this opportunity, and my father, with a combination of gratification and misgiving, gave his consent.

Mrs. Howard had toured Europe, spent several seasons in fashionable London, and had sung as leading contralto with the London Philharmonic, Scottish and Colonne Orchestras, and under Theodore Thomas with the Thomas Orchestra. She was chosen by Dvorak to sing "Biblische Lieder" which he orchestrated for the occasion and came to London to conduct. She was leading contralto at the World's Fair in Paris, where she appeared in Gluck's *Orfeo* as Orfeo with a chorus of twelve hundred voices. She had sung with all the great oratorio conductors of her day in Europe and America, yet she had little personal vanity. She summed up the world rather in the manner of Lord Byron, as something to be conquered and despised. I do not remember her ever reading a book, though she had a veneration for the intellect. It was what she venerated most, the intellect and the arts and graces of life, and for some reason I represented to her just those things. She listened to my every word with a flattering and disconcerting attention.

Every morning an accompanist arrived, and Madame – as she now asked me to call her – taught me the soprano parts from some of the great oratorios.

She used to take me about with her to receptions – dressing me up in some of her own finery, the secrets of which were disclosed to me. Her dearest friend was the wife of a multimillionaire, and it was from her that Madame received most of her beautiful gowns.

One day she took me with her to meet Mrs. Vandervelt – or "dear Lettie," as she called her. Mrs. Vandervelt's house seemed inhabited entirely by butlers and footmen, maids and upper maids, who moved in and out of one's vision, stealthy and inscrutable. She was not a beautiful woman, but she had presence and charm, and owned, it appeared, almost as many costumes as Queen Elizabeth had left behind her at her death. Mr. Vandervelt kept a racing stable and had twice won the Derby.

I used sometimes to dine at their table and to spend the night in one of their palatial bedrooms, with a private bath, and a mute maid to bring me a grapefruit in the morning – scalloped round the edges and as large as a melon.

It is one of the advantages of poverty that the houses of the rich are adventures, dramas into which we enter and from which we escape. It was gratifying to me to think I should be able to impress my family with accounts of the wonderful dinners I attended, with champagne flowing like water, and remarkable people present; though, as a matter of fact, I never met anyone of distinction at Mrs. Vandervelt's house, with the exception of a few popular writers – these being the most sycophantic of people, almost as bad as the sellers of Persian rugs.

Not long after I had known Mrs. Vandervelt, I received a box left by her chauffeur, filled with dresses.

I had always hated dressing up, but when I stepped into these creations, I stepped into another life. Who wishes to conquer in the outward show must follow the rules. It is a game, and games, as soon as we excel in them, become exciting.

There was a costume that the Second Mrs. Tanqueray might well have envied me, as well as a gorgeous opera cloak. I was now armed for battle, yet underneath it was all like something in which I was acting a part, not being exactly false to myself, but leaving all that true life my reading had begun to open up to me, locked away.

It has always seemed strange to me that we can be so deeply involved in events, while remaining so secretly, and even, at times, so calamitously separated from them.

Madame now wanted me to give some return for her confidence in me. She arranged that I should sing at an evening reception where a famous artiste, a kind of American Yvette Guilbert, was to appear.

I was led with my accompanist – hardly less unstrung than myself – into a small library across from Mrs. Fitzroy's ballroom, where the concert was being held. Presently the door opened and the two other performers entered. K.... C....... was a middle-aged woman, with a mass of fair hair girlishly arranged. Her companion, David Bispham, I had often heard sing in opera in Wagnerian roles. His hair was already turning gray and he had something slightly pompous in his appearance. The summons came for me – I was the first on the program – and with my accompanist behind me, I was about to enter the concert room when I glanced round and saw that she did not have the music. I turned back, opened the library door, and surprised Miss C....... clasped tightly in the arms of her companion. It seemed grotesque to me to see this middle-aged woman, a lock of her hair falling over her bare shoulder, and this aging man standing before me as abashed as young lovers. Love-making I had always associated with the young, and yet there was behind the scattered embarrassment of this clever, worldly woman a shy tremulousness, and her companion had been transformed from a strutting actor into a blushing boy. This episode restored in some inexplicable manner my poise, and for long after, my thoughts returned to it. More than anything it brought home to me the essential innocence of sex.

Madame's attitude towards sex was shrewd and disillusioned. She was married to a businessman living in Chicago, of whom she was very fond, and who was devoted to her. She had never asked him a single question that might prove embarrassing, and when he was unfaithful, which happened not infrequently, she welcomed him back with her wonted high spirits and good nature. She told me that Teresa Careno had once said to her: "You and your husband are the only happily married couple I have ever known, and you don't live together." She always consulted his wishes and thought it most generous of him to consent to her going on with her career.

It was delicacy, *finesse* that she adored, and these she associated only with women. She never offended a man. She had no coquetry, no treachery, but she had weapons with which to defend herself. Artists had continually to pay their way to success through the door of a man's sensual gratification. It was said that no singer could attain celebrity unless she was willing to traffic in such coin. Madame robbed sex of all its poetry, all its evil, and all its noble passion, but she recognized it as one of the great forces in the affairs of the world.

Some of my happiest moments were spent walking alone in Central Park at sunset, when the bare, black branches of the trees would stand out against the vivid colors in the sky, and the little pleasure lake, all frozen over, would be like a mirror reflecting now gold, now purple, now grasshopper-green. Often, a late skater would glide round and round in graceful swinging curves.

On one occasion, Courtney, my Paris friend, accompanied me. He sometimes took me out to dinner and the theatre. He was always trying to "place" people, to discover who their parents were. My intensity was dimmed, my confidence in flight. I was attracted to him, but the very look of his languid figure, the cut of his coat, his gloves, negligently held, his immaculate spats made me feel self-conscious, and his conversation was almost as difficult to join in with as would have been that of Mrs. Vandervelt's butler – had he been suddenly endowed with speech. It all perplexed and saddened me. It was as if the young man I had known in Paris was a different person, and this seemed in some obscure way to invalidate life. I felt as if I had been defeated, had lost some indefinable battle.

In the early spring, Madame was anxious to arrange a recital for me and was on the point of taking steps to this end, when a wire came saying that her husband was ill. She at once decided to give up the apartment and go to him. It was in such an atmosphere of shifting plans and abrupt decisions that her life had been passed. Almost simultaneously with her departure and my return to Norfield, another turn of events threw fresh fortune in my path. Uncle Nat had an old college friend who was a famous amateur billiard player and had been chosen to represent America at an international amateur match of billiards to be held in Paris. My uncle decided to cross the ocean with his friend and invited me to go with him. It so happened that my brother-in-law was planning to row in a regatta in Nice in the middle of May, and it was decided that Uncle Nat and I should join him and my sister there, and that I should return with them to Naples.

Chapter VIII

THE GAIOLA

I SAILED with Uncle Nat and his friend, Wilmot Frost, the last week in April, on one of the big ocean liners, the swiftest afloat. Mr. Frost was a large, slow-moving, slow-thinking man, who looked like a farmer and was interested only in sports and stocks. Compared with him, my Uncle Nat seemed a veritable Beau Nash.

The ship was twelve hours overdue, and Mr. Frost had to play his first match of billiards the evening of the day we arrived. He said he felt the motion of the ship all the time he was playing, the table seemed on a slant, and the floor tipped sideways. He lost the match, but was able to blame it so entirely on the captiousness of the table and the unreliability of the floor that some of the sting was taken out of his defeat. This is, I suppose, what the Englishman would look upon as a lack of "public school spirit" in the American.

Paris seemed to hold out no allurements to him, and he sailed back to New York two days after the match.

Nina and Edgar Chad had bought a house, three hours' journey from Paris, and Uncle Nat and I went to spend a night there. It was surrounded by sand dunes, and the sea came almost to the door. Nina was away. We had a delicious supper of onion soup and fresh fish, with the sound of the sea always in our ears. The glowing fire, combined with the kind, welcoming face of Edgar Chad, made my spirits rise as sparks fly up from a bonfire.

We returned the following evening to Paris, and two days later we left on a *train de luxe* for the Riviera. Of our short hours at Nice and Monte Carlo two memories remain strongly with me. One is the expression of the people at the roulette tables watching the turn of the wheel – perhaps the same expression that Turgenev secretly observed on the face of Dostoevsky at the gambling tables of Baden – an expression impassive and feverish, like the look in the eyes of a cat concentrated on a nest of fledglings. The other is the figure of a woman sweeping past us in a state of tragic despair. She was wringing her hands and repeating over and over in long-drawn-out wails: "*J'ai perdu tout. J'ai perdu tout. O, j'ai perdu tout.*" This refrain continued to sound in my ears for long, long after she had disappeared from sight, filling me with a sense of woe and misgiving, as if all one's treasures, palpable and impalpable, might vanish at a breath.

After my uncle's departure, we were driven to the station and there joined Homer's rowing companions – young Italians with a gallantry as native to them as scales to the fish and wings to the bird. It was delicious to hear Italian spoken all round me once more.

Homer and Jeannette were now living on an island at the extreme point of Posilipo, about an hour's ride by tramway from Naples. The Gaiola, as the island was called, was a gigantic rock of volcanic basalt jutting up out of the sea and is believed to have formed part of the Greek colony of Palaeopolis. Remains of the old harbor and town hall were discovered here, and within easy rowing distance of the island was a submerged marble palace, which could at certain tides be clearly discerned. A fisherman would row us to some landing steps that led up to a brick walk bordered by mesembrianthemum – flowers that spread in wild profusion over the island.

My bedroom was in a turret, reached by a flight of marble steps from out of doors. From the wide terrace onto which we came through the long glass doors of the *salotto*, we could look over at Vesuvius, rising to its cone-shaped crater, with Capri gleaming in the distance.

It would be impossible to convey the peculiar magic of life upon this solitary island: how the stars would glitter at night, as if seen from a ship in mid-ocean; how imperceptibly the hours would melt, one into the other, from pale dawn to blazing midday heat, from blazing midday heat to translucent twilight, with the waters lapping over the smoothly worn lava and swishing in and out of the hollow caves. Homer used to rise at six to take a plunge into the crystal-clear water, Jeannette and I following later. We would have our *café au lait* on one of the terraces, then he would call for Federico to row him to the mainland.

Jeannette had a little wolfhound, Bianca, with a coat as white as fanned snow. She had beautiful dark eyes, not the supplicating eyes of the sheep dog, nor the obsequious eyes of the poodle, nor the impatient eyes of the terrier. They were fastidious, stoical, and sad. It was a shock to her when Homer brought home one day a stray mongrel that the children had been stoning in the streets of Naples. This little dog, whom we named Gaillino, as he grew fatter grew also more bold. At the slightest unfamiliar sound he would break into a series of piercing yaps and shrill, prolonged bayings. He had a dusty gray-white pelt and long flapping ears that moved according to circumstance, and his tail was either wagging with good nature or tucked tight between his retreating legs. I, who was fond of dogs, was pleased that he would allow me to make friends with him.

From our island we could see on the mainland a large yellow villa with a cupola. In it lived an Englishman, a Mr. Foley, with his wife and two little sons. Mrs. Foley was a sister of Conan Doyle and a sister-in-law of the author of *Raffles*, a story written, so I was told, in the romantic turret room where I slept. She played the piano, and when she heard that I sang, she asked me to sing to her accompaniment. I looked at her with a puzzled admiration. She had so much knowledge so obscurely hidden away. That is one difference between English people and Americans; the well-bred Englishman self-consciously withholds his social and intellectual spoils; the American, more innocently, and more rashly, throws down his gold pieces at the first sign of a sympathetic response. The Englishman is taught that to open his heart is almost as blameworthy as to run off with his host's silver. The American is taught to be curious and receptive. With the Englishman we are assured of a consideration which, if it leaves us alone as a stray lamb in a blizzard on a midnight moor, does not at any rate assault our private reserves.

I had not been many weeks on the island of the Gaiola when I fell ill with a fever, first diagnosed as Malta fever and later as typhoid. The strain of nursing finally became too much for my sister to bear alone, and a nurse was engaged. Jeanne Krogh was a piquant and charming character – little, slender, and fair, with a pinched, child-like countenance, and hair the filaments of which were as fine as the finest silken floss.

In my lucid intervals I would ask her whether she believed in life after death. "*Ho bisogno di sapere*," I would say in suspense. She would hang her head in silence. Once I had the sensation of dying, of sinking down, down, down. I did not feel fear, but an unresisting serenity. Then the doctor forced some drops of brandy between my lips, and the burning spirits made my pulse flutter, and I came up once more into the gross world that flared across my eyeballs and smote upon my eardrums.

When the sea was too high for us to be rowed to our island, we had to make the crossing by means of an iron swing suspended on a cable. This swing was about thirty feet up from the sea and no wider than a broomstick handle.

One day Homer took his hands for a second from the supports and was pitched down into the turbulent waves, just missing being dashed to death against the rocks. With his famous prowess as a swimmer he managed to land himself safely. Not unnaturally proud of his achievement, he peeled off his dripping clothes and came straight to my sister where she was seated beside my bed, appearing suddenly before her bewildered eyes like a Roman athlete with shining loins, fresh from some gladiatorial victory.

Anyone who has had a long serious illness knows the acuteness of the senses in convalescence, the feeling of being born anew at every moment. My sister brought me some purple morning glories, one day, that transported me. It was as if all the magic of existence were in their petals. It was the same with a bowl of yellow roses. I would immerse myself in their cool green leaves, their pale buds, each scarcely larger than a Malaga grape, and be intoxicated by their fragrance. Now I could be propped up in bed to watch the sun go down each day, balancing like a huge Jack O'Lantern on the edge of the level sea, before it disappeared from sight into the molten waters.

At last the time came for Jeanne Krogh to leave me. I had grown dearly to love this gentle girl who had brought me through so many dark hours. It was not professional kindness, put on and taken off with her uniform, that was the secret of her grace. It was a self-surrender that formed part of her every movement, her every gesture. Many years later, in Mt. Carmel, Palestine, I was nursed through another fever by a Polish Catholic nun – Sister Stanislowski – who had this same quality of natural goodness; and whenever I am tempted to recoil from the inhumanities of man, and to feel doubt of the human race, I have only to recollect the slender figures of these two compassionate women to be reassured.

Chapter IX

LOVE AND DEPARTURE

LIFE on an island can never be monotonous, for the sea gives continual variety to the hours. Sometimes storms would come down upon us, the waves rising higher and higher, hurling themselves against the walls of our house and streaming down the windowpanes. Sometimes we would look out upon a vast basin of iridescent colors, shimmering like the scales of tropical fishes. At night the fishermen would circle round our island, spearing for eels, their flaring torches making luminous pools on the dark waters. Snatches of song in husky voices would be carried to us in the stillness, haunting reminders of the shortness of our days.

Ainsi tout change, tout passe;
Ainsi nous-mêmes nous passons,
Hélas! sans laisser plus de trace
Que cette barque où nous glissons
Sur cette mer où tout s'efface.

As my strength returned, my eagerness for diversion returned as well. My sister was always sensitive to the feelings of those about her, but she lived by an invisible clock within. This was a tendency encouraged by Neapolitan life, for nothing was ever on time in this happy city. There *was* no time. Trains never left or arrived according to schedule; theatres opened by caprice and closed by accident. No one hurried, no one cared. Laborers stretched themselves out in the street or on wide balustrades under the sun, their caps pulled down to shade their eyes. I remember a ball to which I had been long looking forward. Nine o'clock went by, then ten o'clock, and Jeannette had not even gone to put on her party dress. When we did arrive, long after midnight, we were among the early comers.

When you are young, you step into a ballroom as into a fresh element. Russians and Latins are, I think, the best dancers in the world. Anglo-Saxons dance in a responsible, and even in an excitable manner, but the dance is not in their marrow. The ball did not break up until six in the morning, and on our way home we met some peasants going to mass. An old man touched his cap, muttering: "*Eccelenza.*" Two young girls in shawls made a curtsy, and I felt ashamed before them in my mussed ball gown. Peasants the world over concern themselves little, however, with the habits of the gentry. I have sometimes thought their feeling was one of contempt mixed with a deferential cunning. They like to preserve the upper class as effigies, it adds to their amusement.

Sometime in mid-winter I was invited by Mr. Rolfe, the British consul general, to attend an afternoon dance given on board one of the English battleships stationed in the Bay of Naples. Every one of the young officers, when I asked if he would like a war, answered that he would. "And so you actually *like* war?" I asked incredulously. They all replied that life was monotonous at sea, and that war was what they had been trained for. This answer set me thinking. During the war of 1914 this ship, the *Formidable*, was sunk by the Germans, and I remembered these brave young men who had danced so smoothly and spoken so foolishly.

Mr. Rolfe was an imposing-looking man, a diplomat, a gentleman, and a scholar, rather in the tradition of Sir William Hamilton, but without Sir William's waggishness, and without his Emma. He had told me that he had to attend a court dinner at ten o'clock that evening, and as this hour approached I became increasingly uneasy. At last I ventured to suggest that it was surely time to go ashore. The Commander of the fleet, Admiral Beatty, proud as a macaw in full dress uniform glittering with decorations, had just stepped aboard. Mr. Rolfe greeted him as an old friend and then, turning to me, he said with a touch of hauteur: "I never hurry and I am never late," words I have always remembered and tried, I fear, with small success, to put into practice. Hasten slowly – *Festina lente*, as Suetonius expresses it.

Among Homer's acquaintances was an American professor, Dr. Patmore, who had come to Naples to make some studies at the aquarium, where rare specimens of zoophytes and other fish-life were to be found. He and his wife had taken a villa at Posilipo and entertained generously. I met there one evening at dinner a young Englishman called Adrian Clough. He was tall, slender, and dark, with supple muscles and a manner both reserved and responsive. His eyes combined shyness with directness and curiosity with depth. His mouth was sensitive, his hands small, his voice low. Before the evening was over he had asked me to have tea with him the following day.

We met in the Villa Nazionale. I was intimidated because he knew so much more than I, yet all his knowledge was pushed aside as one pushes away an empty glass. Our relationship was awkward, subtle, and exhilarating. It was early in April, and spring was in the bright flower pots at every window, in the expression of the little children, in the very rattle of the carts and the ribbons of the nursemaids. We stopped to watch a man weaving rush seats on some old chairs. He worked with incredible speed, never once glancing up. My companion had the quality of perception that gives to each moment a value. Most people move through life with inattentive eyes. There was nothing that he missed.

Our next meeting came a week later when Mrs. Patmore invited us to dinner and the opera. It was Nietzsche's favorite one, *Carmen.* All the glamour of sex is in this opera, its cruelty, its sensuality, its ecstasy, and its final defeat. As the men stood up and, with opera glasses held in white-gloved fingers, rotated slowly round, staring boldly at the women's bare shoulders, Adrian and I exchanged a swift, intimate glance. Two days later I had a letter from him asking me to lunch in Naples.

We bought some bread and cheese, thinking we would eat our lunch by the sea. At the quayside some fishermen's boats were moored by iron rings to the stone embankment. They were rocking gently on the tide, and we persuaded an old fisherman to take us out in one of them.

We sat eating our bread and cheese in the stern of the boat, with the hot sun shining down upon us. We would have been content to pass the rest of the day like this, but the old man said with some energy that he must get back to his macaroni.

We decided to visit the Capo di Monte Palace, but found the gates closed. Presently an official appeared.

"Have you special passes?" he asked. "This is not a free entrance day."

As he was about to turn us back, I said ingratiatingly, "Ah, what a pity, for the Duc de Gris Chaumont must leave Naples in the morning and he has been particularly looking forward to seeing the famous Capo di Monte china."

The man gave us a deferential stare, then got out his keys and swung open the gates. Adrian said nothing as we walked selfconsciously up the drive. I was piqued. "You didn't approve of my saying that?"

"It was very quick-witted. I couldn't have done it myself."

"Because you're too honest."

"I should never have thought of it. My mind doesn't work that way."

"The crooked way."

Suddenly he burst out laughing. "Where did you ever find such a name? You might have made me a prince, or even an emperor while you were about it."

Some days later I had a letter from him asking me to go to a ball at the German Club, and one from Mrs. Patmore inviting me to spend that night with her.

The ballroom was festooned with garlands of paper flowers, and the floor waxed smooth as a frozen pond. The girls had dainty programs with silk cords and tiny pencils attached. I had never danced with Adrian and expected him to waltz in the manner of his countrymen, but it was more like a Swiss peasant that he swung me over the floor to the strains of *Eternemente*.

He drove back with me through the deserted streets in the early morning light. "I don't know what you think of me," he said.

"And I don't know what you think of me."

"You're a superb dancer. I'm awkward, I know."

"Not awkward, but dangerous."

"It's you who are dangerous."

"No one knows what anyone thinks."

"You wouldn't understand if I were to tell you."

"You evidently think very little of my understanding."

"It's not that," he said with a sudden, strained, almost anguished earnestness.

It was on this note that we parted, and as I entered the Patmores' gate and heard the horse's hoofs sounding fainter and fainter in the distance, I had a feeling of emptiness and misgiving.

Our next expedition was to Paestum. It was now the end of May, and I wore a dress of pale yellow muslin and carried a parasol.

I was very uncultured and viewed the historic landmarks of the centuries rather as I had turned over the pages of my schoolbooks, as if a meaning were hidden somewhere, an extremely important one, but one outside my reach. To appreciate architecture, so I thought, required a special training, a special knowledge, and I was nervous lest my ignorance be shown up before Adrian. When I saw the temple of Neptune, my imagination was aroused in a new way. Perhaps it was the desolation of the surroundings in which it seemed, as it were, to have been dropped and abandoned – the long, parched, scorpion-infested grass and fever-haunted marshlands – that brought home to me in so poignant a manner its serene and classic beauty, and that led my mind back to a civilization that could have conceived and raised up so noble a place of worship.

We had our lunch seated between two pillars, with no one

to disturb us. I thought I had never before known what happiness was, a happiness so delicate, so suspended that I feared to say a word lest the spell be broken. It was as if some understanding, light as air, impalpable yet imperishable, united us in a moment that nothing could ever alter.

On our return to Naples, Adrian signaled a cab and stepped into it after me. When we reached our lane, he told the coachman to wait for him, and we started down the narrow path. He was silent, not even glancing towards me, but it was a silence that seemed to join us in a new and tremulous understanding. As the last turn brought us within sight of the Gaiola, he stopped abruptly as if to say something, but instead he drew me to him and kissed me on the lips, then, turning sharply round, he fled back up the path.

With my blood in a tumult, I went on until I came to Federico's house. He had evidently been watching for me and ran down the steps the moment he saw me.

"*Signorina, Signorina, la Signora ha un bel bimbo!*" he cried out. These words, falling upon me like lightning strokes, drove all else out of my mind.

The birth of my little nephew had come so unexpectedly that even the doctor had not been able to arrive in time, and it was the old peasant midwife that that brought him into the world. The first sound I heard the following morning was his lusty crying. Behind my deep happiness that he had been safely born was a pervasive awareness of Adrian's kiss and the anticipation of seeing him again.

My sister's nurse arrived at mid-day and was rowed over to the island. Hardly had she got on her uniform before a call was heard, and Carlo ran down to the landing step, returning with a bunch of roses. "*Per la Signorina*," he said. There was a letter attached, and I hurried up to my room and tore open the envelope:

> My darling:
>
> I call you so for the first and last time. I must return to England. I leave today for Genoa. I can't explain, but I shall never forget. It is you I shall always love. Pity me rather than blame me.
>
> ADRIAN

I was stunned. All the blood seemed to flow out of my veins, and the hot, still day to lie like an iron weight upon me. He was gone, gone forever out of my life, through all eternity, without explanation, shrouded in mystery, leaving only a few fading petals as proof of our hours together. Life had no bottom, no truth.

Chapter X

RETURN TO PARIS

My sister had decided to return to America for a visit, taking my nephew, the nurse, and Bianca with her. There was a bad storm when we were two days out at sea. People crept along the passageways, wearing life belts, their features pale and tense. One old Italian kept trying to kneel down and stammer out his prayers, a pious feat ending generally in disaster. Fear I seldom experienced in my youth, fear of any tangible peril. Fear of the unknown, I had been long familiar with, but an immediate danger exhilarated me.

I always came back with mixed feelings to my mother's complicated company – her running commentary on events, witty and perspicacious, her sensitive reticent prides, and her spirited unregenerate confusions. I was often impatient, and even merciless with her, but she suffered all, clinging to her views with a combination of tenacious courage and nervous misgiving. She never chided me for my unkindness. At the worst she fell silent and looked sad.

My sister was an example to me at home as well as at school. She and my brother had a peculiarly tender relationship, and she was always charming with my mother. In later years I came to believe that I held a clue to my mother's heart, to her spirit, that made her trust me in spite of my intolerant ways.

Our quality of humor was very similar, and I could say anything to her. She had also a strong sense of justice which she kept like a firm round penny at the bottom of an old purse. She would accept judgments even against herself when her reason was convinced, and she had a loving and forgiving heart.

I had not been home long before I had a letter from Mrs. Howard asking me to come and see her in New York. I found her living on the top floor of a great office building on Madison Avenue. It was the end of August and the heat was intense. The pavements smoked with it, and the noises of the city beat in upon us through the open windows. She unfolded a plan to me. A friend of hers had offered to finance her for a year in Paris while she built up a reputation as a singing teacher and coach. She wanted me to live with her as a show pupil, my expenses to be paid by this accommodating and devoted friend. She was to sail some weeks ahead of me so that she could make the necessary arrangements for my arrival and that of another young girl.

Everything was at last agreed upon, she sailed for France in the middle of September, and I followed three weeks later on the *Majestic*.

There was a dashing young man on board, who walked up and down the decks looking haughtily in front of him, wearing an English suit and avoiding intercourse with the other passengers. It was rumored that he had been an attaché in the American embassy in Rome and had been dismissed because of some scandal. I made up my mind I would become acquainted with him but could think up no way of bringing the desired meeting about.

One day we were writing letters in the library when a flash

of inspiration came to me. Leaning over to him I said in a polite and hesitating voice, "I wonder whether you could tell me how to spell the word *caryatid?*"

He was at once all civility, all attention. He spelled it, and then he said with great seriousness, "How did you think it was spelled, if you don't mind my asking?"

"That is how I *thought* it was spelled," I answered, "but I wasn't quite sure."

The rapprochement had been made by this magical word, for he evidently thought me a unique young lady, indeed, who could be writing home about caryatids. From that moment I was singled out for Mr. Montague's undivided attentions. I would become dizzy walking round and round the decks while he talked in a vigorous manner about his preferences in architecture. I had not the wit to extricate myself nor the courage to confess my ignorance.

Perhaps nowhere in the world are the trivial and the lofty so strikingly juxtaposed as on a great ocean liner. Adrift in this eternal panorama of sky and water, the human cargo pursue their ways – gossiping, gorging, displaying themselves, or sunk in an unseemly torpor. Before I had known Mr. Montague I had used often to walk on the lower deck reserved for third class passengers. Here I could escape from people altogether and go to the prow of the ship and sit against some coils of rope, watching the sailors swarming like monkeys up to the crow's nest, swinging dizzily between the green sea and "the azured vault." The waves, as they washed up against the sides of the vessel, would speak directly to me. It was the true life of the sea.

Madame had taken an apartment on the Rue Greuze, sublet from former occupants, whose crest was on the silver, and whose linen was of the finest. It was furnished with elegance, the chairs upholstered in satin, the floors covered with plush carpets of a pearly hue. Two servants, a cook, and a parlor maid had been engaged to look after us. These rooms, so Parisian in atmosphere, should be regarded less as a home, however, than as the headquarters of a campaign. Though ambitious, Madame was scrupulous and expended her friend's money with foresight and economy. Not a sou was to be wasted; but since nothing succeeds like success, to be successful one must begin by appearing to succeed.

The young girl who was to live with us, to whom I gave the name of Fifirella, arrived shortly after me. Though she had been born in Chicago, she had been educated in a French convent and spoke English almost as if it were an acquired tongue. She was small, with an original and charming countenance, and her large brown eyes expressed fervor and an inquiring innocence. She longed to enter into the sophistications of Parisian life and immediately bought herself a whole wardrobe of new dresses.

Madame obtained from the director of the Opéra Comique, at a substantial sum, permission to use his private theatre in the Rue Chaptal. She then engaged an accompanist, a tall, fair Swiss, called Gustave Ferrari, himself a composer and the accompanist for Yvette Guilbert.

We frequently gave dinner parties, and on one of these occasions there was present the editor of *Figaro*, also the famous prima donna, Lina Cavalieri, with a Russian prince in attendance.

In the middle of the dinner, the editor, M. P. . . . . , fell suddenly silent, a look of deep despondency showing on his features. Nothing seemed to restore his vivacity, and we feared he must have had a recent bereavement. At the end of the meal he leaned over and whispered to Madame that one of his pearl studs had "*disparu*," and would she permit him to remain behind to search for it. Gabrielle, the maid, was told to bring in a screen, and M. P. . . . . was tactfully left by himself. He returned presently to the company, entirely restored to his former sparkling urbanity.

This incident never failed to evoke from Madame peals of laughter. It showed up life as she knew it to be, the fact that a renowned newspaper editor could, by the mere momentary loss of a valuable shirt stud, become as deaf and dumb to the world about him as a child's rocking horse.

My real delights were quite apart from the Rue Greuze. I had come to know an American family called Tiersch – two sisters and a brother, who lived in the heart of the Latin Quarter. They had dark eyes and sloe-black hair and looked like gypsies; and their hearts were given over wholly to the life of art. The oldest girl, Greta, was taking a course at the Sorbonne; Elsa was studying the piano; and Mark, twenty-five, was a painter. Whenever it was possible, I would go to visit them.

This was not as easy as it might seem, for though my working hours were in the morning, when M. Ferrari came to accompany me, Madame kept a sharp eye on my movements because of the obligation she was under to her benefactor. I was not my own mistress, I was an investment, and a doubtful one at that. I was conscientious but unpredictable.

My ambitions were never really centered in a career. I would at any time have preferred to attend a lecture at the Sorbonne with Greta Tiersch than go to a fashionable reception to meet the leading musicians of the day. Madame felt in me this undercurrent of subversiveness. I was like a pony that was being trained to run a race and that was always turning sideways out of the course. As soon as I entered the Tiersches' door, my personality underwent a change. I was as lively as a weathercock in a veering wind. I was considered by them a wit – a reputation due, I fear, more to folly than to the nimble uses of the mind. They could remain in Paris only as long as their money, a legacy from an aunt, lasted. Greta was my particular friend. I accompanied her on several occasions to the Sorbonne.

I would return to Madame feeling guilty and would hurriedly explain that I had been with the Tiersches. There would be an awkward silence. Fifirella's comings and goings were taken as a matter of course. Our tastes differed. She sought out actresses, journalists, men and women who lived by their nerves, their effrontery, and who moved in the bright light of the moment towards coveted goals. I liked seekers after "truth," people of character. I did not mind how eccentric they were. If they could be subtle as well, I rose to the challenge, but it was enough that they should be ardent and sincere.

The event towards which everything was now hurrying was a musical Madame had arranged for me. A talented young American, Con Hamish, was to play the violoncello, and Miss Minnie Tracey, an operatic star just back from an engagement in Geneva, had promised to sing an aria from *Thaïs*. M. Ferrari was to accompany us and to sing some compositions of his own. When Madame told me that she had chosen the Shadow Song from *Dinorah* I was filled with apprehension, but her intention was to display my virtuosity, and this was the aria best suited for the purpose.

The hours I spent with the Tiersches were now more precious than ever, but it was becoming increasingly difficult for me to go to them. Two afternoons before the day of the concert I hurried off, nevertheless, to the Rue Soufflot. Mark Tiersch was there and looked the typical Latin Quarter student, with his velvet jacket, flowing tie, and long coal-black hair. I started up guiltily after tea.

"I'll see you to your bus," he said.

It was a damp, cold April afternoon, and all my misgivings rushed back upon me. When my bus slowed down at the curb I turned to bid good-by to Mark.

"I'm coming with you," he said and followed me up the stairs to the top of the bus.

"I'm afraid," I answered, "you'll find me dull company."

"You can leave everything to me," he replied significantly as we seated ourselves. "I've made up my mind to something, and when I've made up my mind I'm a bold fellow."

"What's that?"

"Before we get off this bus I'm going to give you a kiss. I decided this some time ago, so you needn't protest. I'm from Texas and we're men of action there."

A large snowflake fell upon my cheek, then another upon my knee. The bus turned into the Champs Elysée, and the snow fell faster and faster. The other passengers rose and went below. Mark put his arm about my waist. The snow was seeping down our coat collars and collecting on our shoulders.

After he had kissed me we sat in silence holding hands. I was entranced by the fairy-like scene, the snow lodging in the branches of the horse chestnut trees, as if a shower of white petals had fallen upon them, the bowed figures of the people showing in the diffused glimmer of the street lamps. I had to change to another bus, and Mark remained to see me off. As the bus drew up, I noticed how worn his shoes were and that there was a hole in one of them; and then I took in for the first time, with a stab of distress, that he was without an overcoat.

"*Au revoir*, my little thrush," he said with a gallant smile.

"Good-bye, *dear* Mark."

"I'll give you another kiss for that," he called, as we waved farewell.

Chapter XI

THE DEATH OF A FRIEND

WHEN I arrived home after my ride with Mark in the snow, I was shivering with cold. Fifirella was dining out, and Madame and I ate our dinner in a strained silence. I vowed with a tardy repentance that I would make every effort not to disappoint her.

At the very moment I had taken this worthy resolution, I felt a tickling in my nose and was forced to give a vigorous sneeze. Madame at once knew I had caught a cold. I think she almost suspected I had gone out and caught it on purpose.

I set all my will toward conquering this unwelcome germ. I swallowed pills, rubbed on ointments, and drank a large tumbler of hot lemonade and rum. In the morning I woke with a giddy head, but the tightness in my throat had gone. By the next morning I was entirely restored and could go through my scales with ease, mounting higher and higher, like a trapeze performer swinging to ever dizzier heights, until he sits triumphantly enthroned at the pinnacle of the marquee. It was thus that I held C Major in the treble.

Friday, the day of the concert, was damp as only Paris can be damp. The little theatre on the Rue Chaptal was packed with an audience carefully selected by Madame. Our friend

M. P. . . . . , was there with all his studs in place and a smile dazzingly extended. Con Hamish played a piece by Brahms, and the moment I had been dreading for so long had now come.

I sang some measures a little too rapidly, but otherwise got through the aria without mishap. I had not disappointed Madame. As an encore I chose Schuman's "*Im wunderschönen Monat Mai*," and into this song I poured all the joy I felt at my deliverance. The musical had accomplished Madame's purpose and was reported in the chief journals in terms of praise, and these notices she posted back to her friend in America.

I had no true ambition to sing in opera, but I might have arrived there as a result of Madame's energy and determination had she not suddenly changed her plans. A friend of hers, Mrs. Kennedy, a rich American widow, had rented a château in the country and asked Madame to come and stay with her. With the increasing heat, she decided to give up the apartment and visit her friend. I had made the acquaintance of an English woman, a Miss Murray, who gave piano lessons, and she invited me to share her quarters with her. Through her and other acquaintances I obtained a sufficient number of pupils in English to pay my expenses at this time and to put a little money aside.

The Rue Bailleul, where Miss Murray lived, was a dark, sordid street just back of the Louvre, with a public urinal at the corner. The house had been a children's school, but was now occupied only by the concierge and his wife. There was one large, bare room with a piano, one medium-sized room, which Miss Murray made her living quarters, and at the end of a long uncarpeted passage was my tiny bedroom.

This room bewitched me. The window opened onto a stable

with a cobbled courtyard, and I would see the horses with their arching necks and restive hoofs being taken out to be groomed. The men would sing and laugh and direct glances toward my window.

Perhaps it was the relief I felt at being my own mistress that so beguiled me, and I seemed to enter at last into the true heart of Paris. One could dress as one pleased, and everyone was full of gaiety. The Seine was near, and I would watch the boats pass, and the reflections on its rippling currents, and linger at the bookstalls, where young men with pale brows and old men with knotted fingers fondled tattered volumes. Workers in blue blouses and students in black velvet jackets and wide-brimmed hats cast sidelong glances as I passed. I would bring in delicious little cream cheeses for my lunch, and crisp rolls, and bunches of violets that cost only a few sous.

I had a pupil to whom I went each morning. He was a South American from Montevideo, with a flashing eye and a flowing mustache. He recounted to me the events of his day. At about noon he dressed himself in a smart Parisian turnout with spats and a cane and sauntered up and down the Avenue du Bois de Boulogne, scanning the women as a surveyor might take his bearings. He would go up to the one of his choice and address her graciously, asking her out for a meal. Like Belita, he lived for conquest. I was, so he told me somewhat sourly, the first woman that had passed through his door without being "singed." He would answer my knock, with an old straw hat pulled down over his forehead to conceal his rumpled hair, and a long mackintosh to conceal his nakedness, as he had only just got out of bed. He was, odd as it may seem, entirely free of viciousness. He was, indeed, unusually innocent.

Madame was only a short train journey from Paris, and I went to see her. She hurried me upstairs into her room, explaining in cautious whispers that Mrs. Kennedy, now Mrs. Sharpe, had recently married an Englishman thirty years her junior, a man of doubtful character. He had a mistress staying nearby. This was the gist of the matter, but I was to judge for myself. She then led me down the stairs and out onto the terrace, where tea was soon to be served.

Mrs. Kennedy was a plain woman with gray hair and a severe brow. She might have been the president of a Woman's Temperance Union in a Midwestern American town.

My first impression of Mr. Sharpe was a strong one. I thought he looked like a flashy actor. His face was never in repose, and he moved with a spry and calculated stealth. He tossed off jokes and puns as a juggler tosses balls, one falling fast upon the other, some coarse, some witty, some feeble, some incomprehensible. He frequently ended a remark with the expression "ring-a-ting-ping-pong," as he might have given a last shake to a tambourine. It was by his foolery that he sought to disarm Madame, her sense of the comic being always easily aroused. In our last moments together, as I was being driven to the station behind two bay horses in Mrs. Sharpe's handsome barouche, Madame told me that Mr. Sharpe had a mysterious friend called Clarence. They frequently met outside the château gates. He had been introduced to her once as Mr. Black, Mr. Sharpe and Mr. Black – a good rogue's partnership.

When I arrived back in Paris that evening, Miss Murray handed me a letter. It was from Greta Tiersch telling me that Mark had been injured in a street accident. I hurried immediately to the Rue Soufflot.

There was no answer to my knock, and turning the handle of the door, I entered. The light from a flickering gas jet showed the table set as for a meal, the food cold in the sauce pans. I stood waiting, and presently Elsa came in. I kissed her, and she burst into tears. She went to tell Greta I was there. Greta was pale and composed. Mark had been knocked down by a passing truck and flung against the curbstone. He had been brought home in an ambulance, and the doctor had given him an injection. Greta led me to him. The light from a shaded lamp showed his blue-black bandit's hair against the pillow, his wax-white, gallant features. Presently his eyes turned towards me.

"It's my little song thrush," he said with a faint tremor of the lips that attempted to be a smile. The tears rushed to my eyes.

I remained all night with my friends, doing little services and moving about in that state of benumbed suspension when the heart lies congealed at the bottom of all one's words.

The doctor returned at midnight and gave Mark another injection. He said he was sinking fast. He died at three in the morning.

There is never a moment after a death to dwell alone with our grief. Society flings its demands too heavily upon us — documents to be signed, officials to be visited, the burial to be arranged for, tradesmen anxious for their money. It is natural; for all must live, and to live by the dead is an immemorial trade — a very lucrative trade, death being the one event in the whole of human existence that can be counted upon with certainty. As vultures appear over a carcass, so human beings appear for their pounds, shillings, and pence when the hour has struck.

I did what I could to help my dazed and stricken friends.

This was my first bitter experience of death, and there was something infinitely moving in seeing this brave little home so utterly demolished. With what high hopes, united by their lofty aspirations, brother and sisters had set out to storm the portals of art and letters! The remainder of the girls' legacy had been consumed in meeting the expenses entailed by Mark's death. They had managed to put aside just enough to pay for their steerage tickets home.

I rode with them to the Gare St. Lazare through the crowded sunny streets of a gay Paris morning, with the shop windows full of summer frocks, the cabmen snapping their whips and shouting at each other, and life surging forward at every corner. They had little baggage – a case containing Elsa's piano scores, a wooden box with Mark's paintings, and one small trunk. Just as they were stepping onto the train, Greta slipped into my hand a locket with a photograph of Mark in it. The guards shouted, the doors of the carriages were slammed to, and their pale, resolute faces disappeared from my vision, leaving a great emptiness in my life.

Chapter XII

BARBIZON

Simultaneously with the departure of the Tiersches from Paris, Miss Murray went to England on a visit, and I had the rooms to myself.

I used to go for my evening meals to a little restaurant on the Boulevard St. Michel, called *The Thackeray* because Thackeray had dined there. It was crowded with students. I tried to follow what they were saying, hot thought upon hot thought. They looked as Diderot and Rousseau might have looked in the days of their poverty when they used to meet in the cafés to discuss the problems of good and evil, of love and death. How many faces we see that hint at possibilities never to be realized! I have crept into people's innermost souls as I have sat opposite them in railway carriages or on omnibuses. A woman once passed me in a London street, proud, tremulous, distinguished, with a beauty of the bone and of the spirit – a poet, I thought. Later I saw her photograph in a magazine. It was Miss Edith Sitwell. Grotesque countenances have remained with me as well, floating up out of old experiences; strangers that bring back to me whole portions of my life – people seen at fairs, at taverns, fishing by the sides of streams, selling watermelons from hucksters' carts. The mind is a repository for conglomerate images. They fade away, they reappear; they raise us up, they cast us down.

A German musician, Max Vogler, used to come to see me, and would play Beethoven and Brahms in the big, empty schoolroom, and I would sing songs of Mozart to his accompaniment.

A young American artchitect, called Holland, was also a frequent visitor. He was an enthusiastic disciple of Max Stirner and presented me with a copy of *The Ego and His Own*, which I used to study diligently by the light of a candle. He accompanied me to Chartres one day where he showed a fitting emotion before the celebrated cathedral while I gazed dully up at it. When, long afterwards, I thought of this ancient church with its stiff sculptures and beautiful stained glass, I found that it had remained as embedded in my memory as gold in quartz. It is the imagination that gives meaning to our experience and the imagination seldom acts on demand. It awaits its own mysterious hour.

But it is always the side shows I enjoy most in traveling – the dogs and cats following their caprices, the pale priests in their flying skirts, the old men nearing the end of their long journey, the little children with delicate faces and fleet heels, the young men lolling on the bridges waiting for the girls to pass. All that in new surroundings shows the old recurrent surge of life captivates me.

Late in August, I gave up my English lessons, and having saved enough money to take a holiday, I went to stay at a small pension near Barbizon, where green lawns sloped down to a winding river bordered by willow trees.

A Chinese student was living at my pension and used to fish on the banks of the river, as immobile as a frog under a pond lily leaf. One day I saw him jerk his rod up with such vehemence that the line, with the fish dangling at its end, swung over his head and became entangled in the branches of a tree. "Unga poy-song, unga poy-song," he cried out, half jubilant, half discomfited; and I laughed immoderately at his peculiar accent and his absurd predicament.

This man, who never betrayed by the movement of an eyelash that he had remarked any rudeness, has often returned to my memory to distress me. Years later a Chinese savant sought my aid. He had written a treatise to demonstrate that "the equivalent of the universe is the zero," which few melancholic philosophers would care to deny. He asked me to translate this treatise into English on the typewriter as he read it out to me in French. Remembering my bad behavior at Barbizon, I threw my whole heart into helping this singular metaphysician, whose French seemed almost as incomprehensible to me as his own complicated tongue. As he knew no English, he went off, bland and sanguine, my script rolled up in a beautiful silk handkerchief which he held carefully in front of him in his immaculately gloved hand.

Madame had returned to Paris, Mr. Sharpe having accomplished his purpose and, with a sudden lightning stroke, got his wife, dazed and overborne, to close up the château, dismiss the servants, and leave for some unspecified destination. Madame felt that her old friend was now entirely at the mercy of this unprincipled rogue. "I shouldn't be at all surprised if he murdered her," she said.

Mrs. Sharpe did, in fact, die a few months later under mysterious circumstances. Her death was recorded in a short paragraph in a newspaper forwarded to me by Madame, then in St. Louis with her husband.

I sailed from Boulogne with Fifirella and Madame some time late in October. On board our ship was a famous sculptor, Jo Davidson, who owned a huge mastiff. He used to get this playful beast out from some mysterious hiding place to exercise it, and it would lope, gambol, and gallop up and down the decks, its tongue hanging loosely from its frothing mouth, while the passengers scattered in all directions.

Jo Davidson was a swarthy man with a pointed black beard and a shock of black hair under a small cap. He made his way through conventions as a tramp jostles through a crowd to get to the open road. His manners were casual and his views stimulating.

It was amidst the confusion of custom-house officials, competing taxi drivers, and excited homecoming voices that I bade good-by to Madame. This was to be the last time we were ever to meet, for she became seriously ill some months later with an illness from which she ultimately died.

Chapter XIII

A VISIT TO ENGLAND

IT WILL seem perhaps strange, that after having had so much money expended upon my musical education, and with so promising a future as a singer, I should have abandoned all ambition in this direction. My dislike for singing in public, and the fact that I should have had to build up my musical career against formidable obstacles, still supported by my father, turned me from singing as a profession. Perhaps I lacked the necessary enterprise and perseverance, or they moved in hidden channels. My failures at school, combined with my brother's domination over me, had bred in me a resolution to pursue ends concealed from others.

I had been invited by a friend of Nina Chad's, a Mrs. Leigh, to visit her in London, and my object was now to save enough money to go abroad. I decided to give French lessons, and my mother arranged a room for me where I could have classes and private pupils.

Soon I was busy from early morning until late evening. The society girls wished only to fill up the empty hours and to acquire a culture that could be put on and taken off with their bangles and brooches. My poorer pupils, being stimulated to get their full money's worth, progressed with a fair speed.

I was able to take passage some time in the late winter. On

board the ship was a tall, fair young man with very blue, very honest eyes and something wind-swept and muscular in his appearance. We soon made acquaintance and I learned that he was connected with a labor college in London and that his name was Maurice Stevens. When we parted at Liverpool, we exchanged addreses and promised to correspond.

Mrs. Leigh had a studio in Chelsea near Cheyne Row. She was a little woman with very fine golden-reddish hair, cut in a straight bang across her forehead. She had a skin as delicate as a child's and a beautiful speaking voice. She had painted the miniatures of many famous women of fashion, among them Princess Louise, but she considered this branch of her art a tedious necessity.

She was an ardent theosophist, and huge canvases covered with symbolical figures stood all about her studio, as if awaiting the touch of an invisible spring to start them floating heavenward. She wrote poetry on the same theme, which she illustrated with colored drawings. She was surrounded with books on Eastern religions and used to discourse with me in her musical voice so eloquently that I would find my mind setting sail like a ship into the ether.

She was a lively companion and took the days as they came. We were nourished with bowls of salad, bags of nuts, fruit bought at a huckster's cart, and plenty of cheese and sweet chocolate, and we ate as the spirit bade.

She had many friends, and I went to some parties, where my irresponsible vivacity and irrepressible curiosity seemed to be checked at every turn. Perhaps I had become too used to the Latin temperament.

Each bird has its note, each nation its virtue. When the

Baron d'Holbach came to England, he remarked that the amusements of the people had the air of religious ceremonies, and King Louis Philippe after a visit to London told Victor Hugo that the passersby were "as serious and mute as specters. When, being French and alive, you speak in the street, these specters look back at you and murmur with an inexpressible mixture of gravity and disdain, 'French people, French people.' " Count Caraccioli recounted to his friends that the only ripe fruit he had tasted in England was a baked apple.

I was too young to penetrate beneath the surface. I wondered why people met at all if it was merely to stand and sit like painted images. When a Belgian woman I knew came to England she gazed disparagingly about her and said: "*Où sont tous les beaux garçons?*" She was herself approaching fifty, and conspicuous more for her flaming red hair than for the usual allurements of her sex, yet she had a standard, an expectancy. England was, of course, celebrated for its *beaux garçons*, but, like "the happy hypocrite" in Max Beerbohm's story, they had fitted themselves out with masks, masks of caution and distrust. Mrs. Leigh had a number of acquaintances who revealed, when the masks did drop from them, enough oddities to satisfy all my demands.

Perhaps what I most enjoyed during those weeks was to wander by the side of the river and watch the swans, with their snowy plumage and curving necks, floating down the current, and the reflections on mother of pearl ripples, and to enter into conversations with the old men, seated on benches under the plane trees. For in every city in the world it is always the old men that one discovers on such occasions; their heads packed with memories, their tongues loosened by age, their hours empty before them, they are the philosophers from whom we may learn our ripest, raciest wisdom.

Homer and Jeannette were now living in Bristol, where I went to stay with them. I had always an immediate feeling of liberation in their company – of good times, good food, good tempers, and hours that could be pushed backwards or forwards according to circumstance, and that had, even in a provincial English hotel, something of the gay charm of an Italian holiday.

My nephew had just reached the age when, with the swift agility of a horseshoe crab, he could get himself into the most unpredictable places. He combined this adventurous spirit with a fiery will. Once I detected him in the common sitting room, trying with an impressive pertinacity to bite a piece of the plaster out of the wall where it showed signs of crumbling. My sister sought to divert his attention, at which he set up such a shout that a passing waiter first gave a start, then directed towards us a benevolent, conspiring, extremely English look.

My sister was a charming mother, unpossessive yet tender, unimplicated yet responsible, caught in her own reveries while at the same time treasuring and protecting her babies. I was always happy with her. Homer regarded his English colleagues with his characteristic quizzical and sage detachment. He was never thrown off his balance. He moved through life breezy and unscathed.

I sailed back to America in the early spring. My mother gave me a lovely welcome, but a nervous one. She was fearful lest I should not be happy.

I soon made my room my center, gazing out of my window

at a familiar dogwood tree, with its pale petals that so quickly drooped and fell, immersing myself in my books, and going for long walks in the country with my dog, a pure-bred Boston bull, ferocious when he took a dislike to one of his own kind, but docile enough with his mistress.

I was under the influence of Richard Jeffries at this time and would lie under the branches of some tree, mingling my spirit with its leaves, its sap flowing into me until I was myself a tree. Interwoven in all the memories of my childhood and youth is a consciousness of leaves – leaves coming out in the spring, leaves blazing on the hillside in autumn, leaves rustling under my feet, leaves of every shape and color, dry leaves that the wind would scatter in whirling eddies – maple leaves, horse chestnut leaves, elm leaves, beech leaves, and the leaves of sumac. Now it was spring, and the leaves were as green as the wings of a locust.

I would return home in a state of exaltation and meet my mother's vulnerable brown eye. She was sensitive to my moods – she was sensitive to everyone's moods – but if I tried to discuss my ideas with her, her mind darted sideways. History was to her a collection of shocking and discreditable blunders which had best be ignored. "That dreadful record of crime known as history," as Oscar Wilde put it. Church was a place where a tedious old man, mumbling fantastical incomprehensibilities sent one gradually off to a grateful slumber.

She resembled Mme. du Deffand who, while Mlle. de Lespinasse was reading aloud to her the Epistles of St. Paul, kept interrupting her with the words, "But, Mademoiselle, can you make anything of all that?" My mother could certainly make nothing of it.

As children we all attended Sunday school, and my father owned a pew in the Congregational church, but my mother never went to church herself and would send us off in our best dresses as if undergoing a penance. Sometimes I would steal secretly into the Catholic church to hear the priest intoning in Latin. It seemed all very strange and appealed to my imagination and my dramatic sense.

Class distinctions were marked in our town. There were the old families, the *nouveaux riches*, the humdrum middle class, and the *hoi polloi*. My father had little or no feeling for class, but my mother had a strong one. She could "place" a person by the mere use of a word, the inflection of voice, but her real dividing line was between the vulgar and the refined, the dull and the lively, the orthodox and the original. When my brother said cutting things to me, it pained her; when my father stared accusingly at the food, it troubled her; when I withdrew into myself in mutinous silence, it perplexed and hurt her, but she was an inveterate hedonist and wove out of life the gay conceits that best served at the moment.

My tastes and sensibilities, my suspicious pride, my obstinate and desperate pursuit after some meaning to life isolated me from everyone. Though my reading was so impassioned and so sober, it seemed to my family a peculiar self-indulgence. It was not that I was expected to do any work in the house. We always had servants to do everything. My mother never set foot into the kitchen and would as soon have picked up a beetle as a duster, but girls were not supposed to bury themselves in books and shut themselves up in their rooms. They were supposed to enter into the social life about them and to be on hand at everyone's call.

I frequently went out in the kitchen to talk with our Irish cook, Mary Crowe, who remained with us for over twenty years. Her racy brogue and broad humor and the aroma I got from her of far away places always fascinated me.

Margaret Murphy, our maid, was also Irish, a girl with so sweet a disposition that no word of complaint had ever been known to pass her lips, only occasionally a tear would well into her eye and trickle down her pale young cheek. One evening I found her alone with her young man, Harry. He, too, was Irish, small of stature, with soft brown hair, parted in the middle, and large, ingenuous eyes. His right hand was swathed thickly about with bandages, and he told me that he had caught it in the machinery of the factory where he worked. He would receive no compensation, and if his hand was permanently injured, he would not be employed again.

These facts filled me with astonishment and indignation. The owner of the factory was a respected citizen of our town who lived in a large house and was an assiduous churchgoer. Heretofore my rebellions had centered chiefly in my head. From this moment they entered my heart, for there was something about this young man that touched me. This casual conversation lighted up the whole industrial system for me, it was the door by which I entered a new life.

I decided I would inform myself about our town politics and I persuaded my father to take me with him to some of the town meetings. He was secretly pleased, although my presence caused a stir among the men.

Next I visited the factories. In a hat factory I discovered women working for ten hours a day in the midst of deafening noise and suffocating heat. In one room the thermometer registered ninety-seven degrees Fahrenheit. There were girls barely out of childhood and women with snow-white hair all working as if under a malign edict.

Coming away, I passed some cherry trees, the blossoms running up the boughs and swaying in the breeze, and I felt all the magic of spring ravishing my senses, and in the background, like a sinister shadow, was a vision of the women I had just seen whose lives were being consumed in barren toil. I gave up reading poetry and read books on trade unions, on socialism, on women in primitive society. I informed myself on conditions in the coal mines, the cotton mills, the steel industry; and more and more I came to realize the injustice of our so-called civilization.

Chapter XIV

CONFLICT

AMONG my acquaintances in New York was a woman called Henrietta Rodman. She was surrounded by odd characters – girls who had run away from their parents, women whose husbands had left them, Jewish anarchists, professional beggars of the intellectual order, visiting celebrities, Russian revolutionaries.

Most of these people would come together at the Liberal Club in Greenwich Village with Henrietta in command. Here one could listen to the keeper of a house of ill fame, looking like a prim school teacher, speak one evening, and a pacifist clergyman, looking like a professional boxer, address an audience on the following one.

Henrietta would lead me up to someone and say, "This is Alyse Gregory. Isn't she lovely?" leaving me in a state of extreme embarrassment. She tried to shed about her an air of informality – an informality from which I shrank. I do not mind the rough manners of simple people, and I like the unpredictable manners of ardent ones, but the casual manners of the sophisticated "intellectual" are, of all manners, the most inconvenient to encounter. Henrietta was, however, of a character so noble that I would feel confuted and unworthy.

I used to go to town on a Saturday afternoon and attend the opera or the Russian ballet in the evening, where I stood up through the performance or sat perched in the top gallery, gazing down on the actors, no bigger than puppets. I would sleep at Henrietta's, on an old army cot, wrapped like a papoose in one of her Red Indian blankets. The following day I would have tea at the Liberal Club, where I would meet a disciple of Bakunin, or a Japanese teacher of Jiu Jitsu, or an eminent historian. I would arrive home at night and find a delicious supper ready for me and my mother waiting anxiously to welcome me. My heart would contract and yearn toward her, and at the same time I would withhold myself. Then I would go to bed feeling sad and would lie awake with a heavy conscience and a sense of the incurable loneliness of life.

I decided to start a women's suffrage club and enlisted the help of a girl who had recently graduated from Vassar College. She was more conservative in her methods and altogether of a steadier temperament than I. We succeeded in bringing together at our first meeting six women. One of them, Mrs. Abrahamowitch, was the wife of a Jewish tailor, a stout humorous woman, with a large family of little children. Another was married to a veterinary surgeon. There were two girls from the hat factory, and a lively, intelligent woman who went daily to New York to photograph famous art collections.

To work for a cause, and to reflect in one's silent room on the bitter injustices of human society are two entirely different things. The clear light of consciousness is dimmed as soon as we mingle with others. The intensity with which, behind my newly aroused social conscience, I sought some ultimate truth created in my mind a perpetual confusion. It seemed to me that I only truly lived when in a peculiar and utter stillness my spirit spun over abysses, flew into the empyrean, hovered at the edges of the planet, diffused itself into ether; that I carried with a perilous insecurity some knowledge that might for ever leave me if I gave myself up to public work. My room was my center. It was here that my inner life flowered in a secret suffering and an incommunicable ecstasy. As soon as I set foot out of it I was destroyed, yet it was no longer possible for me to isolate myself, for wherever I went I was pursued by the thought of the injustices of the world.

I began taking long night walks far up on the hills behind my old school, seeking always to penetrate to some meaning of existence, but the hollow night gave back no answer. I threw myself into reading the works of philosophers, but they all seemed to disagree. Schopenhauer encouraged my melancholy, and Gustav Fechner, who influenced me a great deal at this time, seemed to fill the whole universe with whispering voices, so that every grass blade was my dangerous confederate.

> Then did I dwell within a world of light
> Distinct and separate from all men's sight,
> Where I did feel strange thoughts, and such things see
> That were, or seemed, only revealed to me.

The notes of the gramophone would come to me from the room below, connecting me with a world into which I seemed no longer to have any entrance. Sometimes I would open the window, and the stars would fall upon me, peeling my spirit of every mortal illusion. Or I would stare at myself in the mirror until I drew back in fright before the image that gazed out at me – myself that I could never look upon, myself that I could never comprehend, myself that I could never escape, an animal with bright eyes – alone in nothingness, for what is more terrifying to man than his own image?

It was at this time that I began reading the works of William James, and they affected me profoundly. Reality, he said, was only our individual way of envisaging the universe. This destroyed my monistic conception from which I had drawn my greatest inspiration. Later in life I came to feel that we attribute to our moments of prophetic vision an undue importance. The very intensity with which we envelop them about with our dearest illusions, pledging ourselves to remain faithful to them, cuts us off from other visions, other possibilities. This holds true of the sensitively cherished presumptions of the idealists as well as of the toughly defended ones of the materialists.

Nina and Edgar Chad had come to New York and taken a studio, where I met one day a bland, slow-speaking man with an air of languid intellectual superiority. He was a student of Freud (who had not yet been translated into English), and it was from him that I first heard the name of this great man.

I got into an argument with my new acquaintance, and he directed all his logic (that nimble game of intellectual leapfrog that the Greeks used to regard as an exercise for schoolboys) at me. He seemed in some way to side with my family, to make me feel that I was peculiar and that what was most real to me – my inner life – was a kind of fanciful retreat, where, "*caressant avec extase une rêve intérieure*," I escaped altogether from the world. He told me that there was very little that was not known, and that if we understood ourselves, we would find life "a very tolerable affair."

I went home in a state of excitement that kept me from sleeping most of the night. Yet mystery was still everywhere about me, explained but inexplicable. The fact that we had evolved from the primordial ooze did not make an eyelash any less confounding or a morning-glory any less miraculous. My pulse that never stopped its beat, the white pigeon that flew past my window – were they not symbols of some ultimate mystery on which all life floated and that could never be known?

My mind was in a dire confusion, seeking truth as a man in prison seeks a way out. My nights were filled with a piercing knowledge of the cosmic mysteries surrounding me, as if death were about to devour me – a death that did not hold the assurance of oblivion even, but suggested new and nameless frights. It seemed monstrous to have been dropped helpless and unapprised into a universe without explanation and without purpose.

I could still, however, emerge from "the dark night of the soul." Indeed it has often convinced me of the incorrigible frivolity of the human intelligence that we can alternate so quickly from one state to an entirely contrary one.

Among my acquaintances was a young English actor who was taking a leading part in *The Passing of the Third Floor Back*, then having a long run in New York. I would arrange to meet him at the exit of Carnegie Hall after the Sunday afternoon concert. My head still dizzy and exalted with the strains of the music, I would see him, a figure of fashion outlined against the black track of the elevated railway. He wore a top hat, imperceptibly tilted, a smart afternoon coat, striped trousers, suède gloves, and he always had a flower in his buttonhole. He was everything that a famous actor should be.

We would walk in Central Park or stroll through the Metropolitan Museum of Art, where he would bring out an eyeglass to scrutinize the pictures, squinting at them with an ambiguous earnestness and then backing away with an air of judicial discernment. We would go to the Plaza Hotel for tea, and as I caught the first strains of the orchestra playing a waltz of Delibes, I would feel a surge of capricious excitement, entirely separated from my deeper insights. He had eyes as hard as onyx, that would melt and become as soft as the petals of a black pansy. He would use me as a mirror to see himself shining back enhanced. Then I would leave him, and my true life would surge up within me, and the menace of infinity press upon me, and I would feel more than ever lost.

Chapter XV

CAMPAIGNING

The Scottish socialist, Keir Hardie, had been advertised to speak at a nearby town, and I went to hear him. He was a gaunt old man, with the white hair and beard of a Biblical prophet and a strong Glasgow accent. His speech was simple, logical, and moving; but as I glanced about me at the faces of the audience, I felt a sudden, withering uncertainty, as if I were with people alien to me, who, if given power, would use it to destroy what I held most dear – great works of art, the music by which I lived, the gracious fruits of an ancient and elaborately evolved civilization; as if the whole world might easily turn into one vast horror of aimless, tasteless, triumphant mediocrity. Could the things I valued be preserved only in a corrupt society? I left the hall profoundly shaken.

In the end I was thrown back on my memory of Harry's face and the girls at the hat factory. It could be nothing but shameful to participate in a society where some were slaves and others free. Perhaps it was necessary to sacrifice the best in man in order to obtain the well-being of the greatest number.

Some days later a young woman called to see me and asked me to join a group of girls working to obtain the vote in our state. I was to be at a certain place, prepared to make a speech, in a week's time. I rushed up to my room to compose the speech, my head full of ideas.

I was soon swept into a new life where all fanciful reflections were carried from me like a leaf in a swirling torrent.

Of my working companions – there were five of us – Lucy was petite, with a heavy coil of shining black hair that seemed to weigh down her small, bird-like head. She combined sophistication with zeal. She and I usually addressed socialist and trade union meetings.

Eleanor was from Utah, where women already had the vote. She was a large, handsome girl of an extremely sober demeanor. When I asked her about the Mormons, the very word caused her to change color. "It's too terrible to talk about," she said.

Cornelia was my special companion, and we formed a lasting friendship. She regarded everything about her with a humorous and enviable detachment. She had soft skin, soft hair, and eyes quizzical and kind.

Brenda was the Commander. She was the most indomitable person – man or woman – I had ever encountered, and I was secretly nervous with her. Suave and satirical, impassioned and discreet, with an intelligence that was lucid, imperious, and astute, she could work the clock round without betraying a tremor of fatigue. Men's vanities and "trickeries" were the continual butt of her mordant mockeries. Disarming and propitiatory on the surface, she was enflamed by injustice, cruelty goaded and hardened her, and revenge was her secret weapon.

Her inexhaustible enterprise and statesmanlike ability made her a formidable foe to the politicians that were our enemies. Thanks to her, every town, city, and hamlet now had its suffrage league. School teachers, actresses, conscientious mothers, beautiful young girls, workers from the factories, all came forward to help. There was a new ardor among women that ran through every class. It liberated their minds and broadened their sympathies, gave hope to the oppressed and courage to the unhappy.

The first suffrage parade in which I marched was in New York City. The crowds – a vast ocean of incredulous, surly masks – were banked up on the sidewalks, hanging out of the windows, and perched on every available fence. We felt that we in our generation were taking our place in that age-old struggle of enlightenment against ignorance, of liberty against fatality. The men, a tiny band, embarrassed but valiant, brought up the rear and were loudly hooted and hissed. No woman who has fought for the emancipation of her sex will ever forget the men who supported and encouraged her at that time.

As a rule, men's attitudes towards women have varied little throughout the ages, and may be said to fall within simple classifications. There are those who, frustrated in love, turn the weapon of their wit into an instrument of spite and retaliation, thus seeking to restore their wounded pride. Nietzsche and Strindberg may be given as examples of this type. Others, seeing clearly the advantages to their sex through the continued subjugation of women – advantages whereby they have at their command a willing servant, a conciliatory wife, a resourceful mistress – hold with obstinacy to their supremacy. Schopenhauer was one of these.

Rarest of all have been those men whose magnanimity and passion for justice have caused them to see in the tyranny of man a desire to retain a dominance unworthily secured, and in the stupidity and predatory fierceness of woman the results of a mind shut away from growth and a body given over to a round of exhausting and uncreative work. Voltaire, John Stuart Mill, and in our own day, Lord Russell are in this sense eminent.

Perhaps woman has always been to man an uneasy extension of his own dreads. In each age she is his latest invention. Women use their power over men when and how they can, sometimes without mercy; but men hold the key to the world's spoils, to the exciting adventures, to the honors and high positions and high salaries, and they intend neither to share this key nor – how monstrous indeed! – to give it up.

All life is warfare, "a bow bent in battle," but with men and women the issue is confused by the bitter-sweet, sharp-tender duel of sex, this heady elixir with its fatal drop of mandragora which the unwary swallow with so avid a thirst. I have never felt resentment towards men. Indeed I have often felt sorry for them. I judge them as individuals, as friends, as lovers – by their intelligence, their courtesy, their good nature, and their good-looks. It would be easy to be as rude at their expense as they have been at ours, and even easier to be as witty, but it would end only in being as dull:

> I am much sorry, Sir,
> You put me to forget a lady's manners,
> By being so verbal.

I am more incensed by those women who hang like dead weights around the necks of men, who cling to and exploit their privileges, who retard the advance of other women and throw dishonor on their claims, than I am by men, who, like a lot of nervous smugglers, are hardly to be blamed for fearing their booty may be snatched from under their very eyes and their suppers left to sizzle and scorch on the kitchen stove:

> Yet with my nobler reason 'gainst my fury
> Do I take part: the rarer action is
> In virtue than in vengeance.

What a vision of society came to me in those breathless, driven days – its inequalities, its pretense, its squalor, and its unrecorded crimes! Men and women with sallow, joyless countenances, sucked into great factories as into the jaws of a dragon, bludgeoned by noise, grappled to machines, shambling in and out of five cent shows, eating bad food, sleeping in badly ventilated rooms – and time passing, passing, passing, the stars shouting a warning they were too stupefied to heed. The proud merchants, brisk and complacent, counting their money, lolling in their stuffed chairs, filling their houses with grotesque ornaments and their heads with nothing at all, smoking big cigars, swinging golf clubs over corpulent bellies on Saturday afternoons, with tiny little boys trudging wearily in their wake, lugging enormous bags with their gear, and above them the stars, too, shining in vain.

Perhaps what was most reassuring was the intellectual hunger of young people in the small towns.

When allowed to do so, we would go through the factories. In cotten mills the girls were all young, and their pale, grave faces would look up at us with a mute appeal. They received five dollars a week for a ten hour working day, and many had consumption caused by breathing in the fluff from the looms. One of these workers, Florence, attached herself to me, a fair gentle girl who had already begun to cough with the malady that in the end killed her. She used to attend my evening meetings and return with me to our hotel, and for more than a year her letters followed me about, scrawled in a childish handwriting, becoming more and more pathetic. Her face, like that of Harry was forever burnt into my heart.

In the spring we stayed in small country villages where life had the immemorial charm of such places the world over. I would feel a delicious sense of pleasure as I drove in the fresh morning air up and down the winding, hilly roads between apple and cherry orchards, past old Colonial houses and little churches with pointed steeples and cemeteries grown over with long grass. Eleanor and Lucy had left us, and two new girls had taken their places.

Ann was intellectual, with hair the color of faded bracken, and curving Mona Lisa lips. She intended to become a doctor. Freda[1] was slim, with a boyish figure, dark eyes, and teeth that flashed like an Ethiopian's. She had something of the *gamine* about her and was in perpetual high spirits.

When the feeling was so strong that we could not secure a hall, we would hold our meetings on the village green, and farmers and their families would drive from all the outlying districts to hear us. We were continually being asked to repudiate the English militants, but this we refused to do, losing supporters in consequence. We were all in sympathy with the English suffragettes and had adopted their colors as our own.

In the early summer we disbanded and I organized a suffrage play, traveling with it to some of the fashionable seaside resorts.

[1] Freda Kirchwey, now editor of the *Nation*.

Our first performance opened at the beautiful old town of Saybrook. There was a dance after the play, but before getting into bed, I stole off for a swim. Sea bathing at night has always seemed to me full of magic. Perhaps it is that we experience life more intensely when we catch it off guard.

In the autumn I followed the country fairs. This I did by myself. Next to my booth was a man who sold buttons with inscriptions: "Meet me tonight," "You're a Daisy," "Will you be my Sweetie?" He presented me with one of his buttons bearing the cryptic word ISHKABIBBLE. I gave him in return a "Votes for Women" button, which he pinned carefully under the lapel of his coat. He was a droll fellow with a dusty, sandy-colored mustache and little sagacious eyes. He looked upon the cause for which I was so earnestly pledging my days as a kind of whimsical madness and my booth as a comical side show. He had himself never voted and would undoubtedly have taken immediately to his heels had he been asked to do so. He laughed at me and I laughed at him, and we derived continual amusement from one another.

I came to know on friendly terms, as a sharer in the vicissitudes of a mountebank's life, the clowns and acrobats and other trailers after the fair. The snake charmer was a handsome Roumanian girl, who said she had always been a suffragist. She had an enormous cobra which coiled itself around her arm with its head held menacingly up. She assured me that it was harmless and allowed me to touch it. It had a beautiful texture, firm and smooth. I at last took to borrowing it. I would put it in the deep pocket of my coat, where it would lie in a heavy coil, like a sailor's rope, and when someone began to be truculent, I would draw it out, saying apologetically: "My snake needs the air." I do not, as a rule, care for practical jokes, but I met some very unpleasant people.

I slept at home during the last week of the fairs. I used to be exhausted at the end of the day after standing for so many hours with the noise dinned into my ears and the arguments always the same. Then I would get into my car and drive over the silent country roads, and as night fell, I would hear the bark of a dog, now faint, now loud, as I passed a lonely farm house, and all my serenity would return to me. The car would seem to have wings, so swiftly did it glide through the mysterious night.

After the fairs broke up, I had a week's vacation and I went to spend it with my brother in his country home. I used to love the autumn there, always my favorite season, with the leaves turning to scarlet and gold, and bittersweet bordering the roadside, and oldman's-beard festooning the woods, and fluff from milkweed seed blowing into my face and floating away over my head.

There was hardly a town or village in the state where I could not be certain of receiving a welcome from some sympathizer with our cause. I frequently stayed in a charming old house in Wallingford, with an elderly lady and two old gentlemen, very like figures in a Henry James novel. Indeed the house might itself have been lifted straight out of *The Spoils of Poynton.*

It was a little sanctuary of old gallantry and generous idealism; their courtesy was so delicate, their humor so glancing, their tact so faultless. Perhaps I might have been speaking at a motion picture house between reels or addressing a street meeting of turbulent rowdies, but the moment I set foot over the threshhold of their door, I knew no harm could reach me.

In a mountain village on the border of the state, I was often the guest of an original and attractive woman, married to an architect with a long, black, silky beard and ironical eyes. Their house was an enormous one, with lofty ceilings, rough white-washed walls, and rooms that were like medieval halls with vast open fireplaces where great logs would crackle and blaze half through the night. I would sink into my bed as into a cloud and watch the shadows flickering up on the ceiling and feel deliciously separated from my usual self.

Behind all the vanishing days my deepest thoughts kept their hiding places, unexpressed and inexpressible. On my train journeys I would sometimes look out of the window and see the squalid approaches to some town, the staring advertisements, the straggling hovels, the ugly factories, and my eyes would avidly search the horizon where the sun was setting, the sky on fire, and suddenly all my efforts would seem in vain and the true secret of life forever withheld from me.

Chapter XVI

NEW JERSEY

THE State of New Jersey was to have a referendum on woman suffrage, and I was asked to go there as an organizer. I was now only a short ride by tube from New York and I would frequently spend my week ends with Cornelia, who lived in an alley in Greenwich Village, in a little old brick house. I would arrive late and weary on a Saturday night, and it would be delicious to wake in these quiet rooms, with the leaves of the ailanthus trees casting spidery shadows outside the small square windows:

The ailanthus is my tree. Her buds are jets
Of greenish fire that float upon the air.
They set my feet upon a Fosse-way, where
Old mills turn mossy wheels and wide sunsets
Redden the outstretched wings the heron wets
In old ponds that the day and darkness share.
Candles they are, that on a wayside bare
Re-gather what the human heart forgets.
Green lamps they are, whose life-sap sweet and strong
Brims from most brittle and most tender wood.
They leave their dusty branches. They float over
The houses and the roofs, a wild-goose throng.
High up they fly, a thin free multitude,
Leaving their earth, their roots, their twigs, their lover!

Later when I came to live under the shadow of one of these trees I could appreciate the charm of these lines by Mr. John Cowper Powys.

I had, shortly before joining Brenda's campaign, come upon an essay in the *Atlantic Monthly* on friendship, by Randolph Bourne, whose name was then unknown to me. In it he referred slightingly to women's friendships and disparaged solitude. I wrote him a letter defending both women and solitude and received soon afterwards a reply. "I should like to know more about your ideas on people," he wrote. "I am interested in nothing else, and all my studies are valueless except as they throw light on people's souls and personalities." We arranged a meeting at which I discovered him to be a hunchback. He had a fine intellectual forehead, blue eyes of extraordinary intelligence, ironical and childlike, and long, slender, nervous hands in which one could almost feel the pulse beating. I had been so delighted by his exciting mind that I felt, after leaving him, as if my life had taken a new turn.

He had received the Gilder Fellowship from Columbia University, which enabled him to spend a year of study and travel abroad, and during this interval we kept up an animated correspondence. When he came back to New York, I arranged to meet him one afternoon in Central Park and go with him to his rooms for tea. There I was introduced to his friend Max, a tall, fair Austrian with whom he was living, a follower of Kropotkin and a connoisseur of old engravings. I was enchanted by that tea and felt as if the light of the mind and the graces of friendship could redeem the most strained existence.

I was given a car, with two girls to assist me in my work, one of them a beautiful Jewish girl called Rebecca who was observant of the beauties of the countryside, and of all the little incidents that lent drama to the hours. Our work carried us into every corner of life. On one day I would be speaking before a policeman's convention where the men were roaring tipsy on beer, on another, before a fashionable whist drive. I spoke at prisons, at fairs, at liquor saloons, at church suppers, at movie houses, at the doors of factories, at trade union halls, at public banquets, at clam bakes, before friendly crowds and hostile crowds, in town and in country. We spent two weeks at a fashionable seaside resort where millionaires and their families came for their midsummer holidays. The wife of a noted banker contributed generously to our treasury. With her help I got up a suffrage parade, which she led in her car.

The place filled me with depression. It had none of the quality of a natural port, with fishermen pulling in their boats and nets lying out to dry. Everything struck the eyeballs like a blow – the dazzling roads, the glaring houses, the metallic faces – but there was always the sea.

No matter how late we returned to our rooms, I would steal out to have a last look at the sea before getting into my bed. In the daytime it seemed to have been taken over, bought up, as it were, for cash, but at night it was what it had always been.

All restless desires, all human thought, seemed to dissolve against the eternal rhythm of its surge and fall, and behind all the strain of these feverish days its murmur kept coming to me as a message of hope on the summer breeze.

My suffrage experience developed in me an immunity in the face of crowds. At the bottom of all my encounters I was conscious of something that isloated me. I used to recover my purpose by thinking of the men and women in the past who had made possible by their courage the freedom I was now enjoying. When in our hours of bitter discouragement we are apt to lose confidence in the human race it is well to recall the liberties we have won that are still with us.

How familiar I grew with the look of the city streets late at night, where only tramps, drunkards, and the disinherited were lurking in doorways or moving stealthily, aimlessly, hopelessly over the hard asphalt. In the country a man may get off by himself and howl like a dog, or he may fall down and bury his head in the unaccusing grass. No one will molest him, no one will ask him any questions, but in these thoroughfares of granite he must keep upright, he must step forward, he must go somewhere, do something, be somebody. If he has a mortal illness, or a mortal anguish, he can carry that with him.

We would be famished after our late meetings and as there was no restaurant open, we would go to the hot-dog wagon, a kind of caravan where hot 'Bologna' sausages, smothered in mustard, were served. This was long before I had become a vegetarian. How much inconvenience we might save ourselves were our imaginations less active; although the immemorial practice of slaughtering animals for food has never seemed comparable to me in the gruesome to the calculated, scientific experimentation on animals that is honored with the name of "laboratory research" and is the singular prerogative of "superior man." I am here in agreement with Bernard Shaw.

The newspapers were, on the whole, favorable to our cause, and we were confident that the referendum would be carried. We were allowed, with the anti-suffragists, the right to watch at the polls. I was stationed in one of the poor sections of Newark where there was a dense population. All day brutish-looking men would be marshalled up to the voting booth, many arriving in motor cars, some barely sober enough to keep on their feet. "We've come to vote against the ladies," they would say with a leer. They had been raked out of back alleys, saloons, gaming-dens – everywhere and anywhere – to defeat us, and they were successful. It was a lesson I never forgot, and at the moment it made me feel hopeless about all social reform.

Chapter XVII

A VOYAGE

I HAD been saving my money with the intention of going abroad and had engaged passage in a ship sailing for Norway, from where I meant to cross over the North Sea to England.

I had allowed some days to see my friends in New York, and among them was a young man called Clyde, who looked like an early Viking, and who was fired with a lively sense of moral responsibility. He would come frequently to my meetings and make speeches for me. I would see his fair head and broad shoulders rise up out of the crowd and feel an immediate sense of pleasure. I had gone to his rooms for tea when he was still a student at Columbia, and there I had met a friend of his, Gareth Channing, to whom I was attracted. Now, when I called Clyde on the telephone, it was Gareth who answered. Clyde was out, he said "But I'm here. Won't you have dinner with me?"

He came for me at Cornelia's. It was the last day of October. He suggested taking me to a Syrian restaurant near the Battery, and we decided to walk. I felt with him like a bird that has flown from one climate to an entirely different one. There was something unpredictable about everything he did and said.

The restaurant was in a poor section of the city, but the food was adventurous, and we enjoyed looking at the unusual people with their slanting eyes and olive skin and animated, incomprehensible conversation.

After our dinner we walked to the end of the Battery and watched the ferries coming in, the great cart horses straining at their bits, tossing their manes, and bringing each hoof down like a thunderbolt.

Not since I had been with Adrian had I felt so attracted to any man.

We turned back and wandered through streets with skyscrapers rising like canyon walls on either side of us. "Shall we go in?" Gareth said, pausing before one of them. The night watchman took us swiftly up through the silent offices, which were like deserted hives. Gareth led me up an iron staircase and out onto a stone balcony, where we stood as if in mid-space between the glimmering stars and the firefly lights of the city beneath. He put his arms about me and we kissed as lovers.

The next day I went home to bid farewell to my parents, for I was sailing the following afternoon. My father feared I might never return, as it was during the first world war. Clyde came to see me off, arriving at Cornelia's in time to go with me in a taxi to the ship. It was his figure I saw above all the others in the crowd, he was waving his black felt hat in the pale November sunlight.

There were few passangers making the crossing: two unhappy German women returning to their country, a professor of biology, with original views, who said he never cared for women until they had passed the age of thirty. There was one man who never addressed a word to anyone during the whole twelve-day voyage and who was sometimes seen swinging his arms in a mysterious fashion on the tcp deck – as though to confederates hidden in the clouds.

At the Hebrides a passenger was hauled aboard by a rope, a

poor, terrified-looking man who was kept in confinement. Once we were all rushed down to the dining saloon and black curtains fitted over the portholes.

Christiana, where we landed, was blanketed with snow. I drove to a hotel, arriving just in time for dinner. There was a table reaching the length of the room, stocked as for a royal banquet – jellied meats, caviar, *pâté de foie gras*, cheeses of every variety, and a bewildering assortment of other viands. The guests took their plates to this table and helped themselves, and since this was only in preparation for the meal to come, I judged that Norwegians must have hearty appetites and sound digestions.

That night the murmur of voices was carried to me through the open window as I lay unable to sleep, suggesting gay, intimate hours, and I felt suddenly as if there were nothing to give life value.

The next morning this fainthearted mood had entirely vanished and I was eager to be out early. The streets were swarming with students, all mounting over the hard-packed snow towards the university. How different they looked from French students! These young men were spare and hardy and not given, if one could judge from appearances, to weighing too closely the imponderable essences of intellectual equivocations. In the museum I saw some Viking ships, dating from the eleventh century, that had been dug up in the neighborhood. They so fired my imagination that I later obtained a history of these fierce people, so fierce that a special prayer was inserted in some of the litanies against their savage visitations – *A furore Normanorum libera nos.*

I left Christiana for Bergen on an early morning train. In

the compartment with me was a young man, dressed in knickerbockers, with a chestnut mustache and little bright observant eyes like a squirrel's. Presently he offered me some fruit, and I discovered he was an Austrian returning to serve in the army. He told me he thought no cause worth fighting for but that of pleasure, and the only conquest meriting attention, that of love. He discoursed eloquently to me on the women of his preference – their nationality, age, and complexion. "And what men do you prefer?" I inquired. "I don't care for any, they are all my rivals." He had been traveling in many countries because his mother said it was better to see the world than to go to war.

For long periods I would stand looking out at the villages in their snow mantles, the farms perched dizzily on the mountainside. Traveling in trains has never lost its romance for me. The very sound of the whistle of an engine can excite my imagination. There is the wild dragonlike whistle of the American engine, evocative of great prairies and wide spaces, and there is the screech of the Swiss engine as it turns a hairpin bend on the side of a perpendicular slope. I could almost tell what country I was in by the whistle of its engine.

It was dark by the time we reached Bergen, and I discovered that I must leave there the following day, as it was uncertain when another boat would be sailing for England. Ships were being sunk continually on this route.

The steamer I boarded the next morning was the smallest seagoing ship I had ever been on. At that age I loved the feeling of a ship, even its slippery decks and flapping canvas and creaking ropes. I thought I had never seen a more beautiful harbor than that of Bergen, with its picturesque fishing smacks and timber ships dotting the water, and the town rising up behind, gleaming in the sunshine. I felt all the delights of an irresponsible traveler, forgetting the dangers that might lie ahead. The ship was manned by English sailors, and the mere sight of an English sailor is always enough to allay one's fears.

We sailed off serenely, though the sea was choppy. There were, as far as I could determine, only three other passengers, all men. One of them was large and powerfully built, with a thick golden beard and a fur cap pulled down over his ears. He stood clinging to the rails of the ship, staring towards land until it had disappeared entirely from sight; then he began pacing round the decks with long strides.

Presently the sea began to get up, and by the time the lunch hour had arrived, there was a gale blowing. Only one passenger, beside the bearded man and myself, came to the table, a morose-looking individual with tightly sealed lips, and eyes that concentrated inwards.

The steward, as he was about to serve us, was flung back and was barely able to hold his balance. "You are brave, Mademoiselle, to risk the voyage," said my neighbor, whom I discovered to be Russian.

The steward made a fresh effort to place the dishes in front of us, but this time the ship heeled in the opposite direction, thrusting him against our chairs and causing him to spill some hot soup over the morose man. "Sorry, sir," the steward said in his most respectful English manner.

"*Ce n'est pas agréable*," the Russian remarked to me, and it was this observation, combined with the embarrassing predicament of the steward and the almost pathological impassivity of our traveling companion under rude surprises that set me off laughing. The Russian laughed, too, a hearty, sonorous laugh.

It was Aristotle, was it not, who defined the comic as something "out of time and out of place without danger"? But here the danger was not lacking, and even to reach my stateroom after my difficult and imprudent meal was a feat requiring perseverance and ingenuity.

I lay in my berth, my knees braced against the wooden boards, feeling sick and giddy. All through the night the ship tossed up and down, sometimes seeming on the point of foundering, and then, with a vibrating, shuddering strain rising once more, while the wind whistled and shrieked and pounded against the portholes. I remembered a description I had read of Lady Hamilton nursing her husband and Lord Nelson through a storm at sea and wondered whether it was as bad as this one.

The book I had taken with me was one by George Gissing, called *Will Warburton*, the only book by this author I have read. I held to it as to a talisman against destruction, so remote did its story seem from the elements that roared and swirled about the insubstantial boards that housed me.

By the morning the storm had subsided, and by the time we came to dock at Newcastle, in a drizzling rain, there was only a slight swell. I noticed, as the gangplank was about to be lowered, a girl straining anxiously forward. Suddenly she gave a shout of joy and frantically waved her arm. I glanced round to see whom she was greeting in so extravagant a manner and to my surprise I saw the morose man so transformed as to be hardly recognizable. And as they rushed into each other's arms, I reflected upon this magical force that can make the wicked good, turn fear to trust, misery to rapture, and darkness to the most radiant light.

Chapter XVIII

ENGLAND IN WARTIME

IT WAS a general desire for adventure, and anticipation of seeing my sister and my friend Maurice Stevens, with whom I had been corresponding ever since our parting at Liverpool, that had brought me to England at this critical moment. It was he who had found me a place to stay near Kensington Gardens.

He was a strong conscientious objector and argued with so much logic that my natural pacifist leanings were fortified. I did make an effort to join a unit of women who were being sent to Serbia, but was rejected because of my foreign nationality.

If I could qualify in no such capacity, I was determined to learn all I could about British institutions, and Maurice obtained permission for me to go down into a coal mine. With how little imaginative insight had I visualized these dungeons of woe! The men accepted without complaint, apparently, their long hours of darkness, damp, and danger. They were intelligent, friendly men, who led us through the endless mazes of tunnels by the light of their miners' lamps. We came upon a pony, which, I was informed, was not taken out of the mine until it was too feeble to be of use. This pony with its flowing mane and deft hoofs and wildly beating heart had been cunningly captured on the Shetland moors, never again to feel the free wind on its sensitive hide, or to nibble the fresh, green grass of spring. Pit ponies become eventually blind.

Maurice was not my only cicerone in London. I had known in my Paris days a young Englishman who had given me his card, and I now sent him a note. He was a captain in the army, on leave at the moment, and free enough to take me out to dinner and the theater.

Captain Hawarden had all the *savoir-vivre*, all the assured arrogance, and all the mental sluggishness of the ruling class. He was rich, debonair, and handsome, but ideas were less to him than icicles to cats. He was the kind of young man who would have asked nonchalantly for a match to light his cigarette as he was being stood up against a wall to be shot. It would never have occurred to him to inquire what he was fighting for, or what he was dying for; and he was as indifferent to the inequalities of society as a peacock to the quantum theory. He would judge Maurice from a purely class point of view, and Maurice would judge him from a purely moral one.

How impossible it is to come to conclusions! This young man represented both the best and the worst in human society. He would be reckless in action and brave in death, and would throw his life away for his country, right or wrong, almost as lightly as he jumped onto the running board of his motor car; yet if I had persuaded him to go down into the mines with me, he would have shaken the experience from him as a dog shakes water from its back. His sole concern would have been where we could get the best lunch.

To Maurice I was genuinely and loyally attached, but my most dizzy thoughts were now centered upon Gareth back in New York. We would walk, Maurice and I, in Kensington

Gardens, and he took me to some of his socialist meetings and introduced me to his friends.

Mystery was always pressing in, life was always escaping. Was Maurice right, and would a different system of society create a world in which justice ruled and all might seek fulfillment in security? Or would the morbid ambitions of men, dark in intention, faulty in intelligence, and pitiless in action, still find some means of trampling on happiness?

My mind is a divided one, causing me to swing from one view to another according to the intensity of my vision and its direction. Maurice's mind maintained its steady and consistent course. He felt the deepest contempt for the socialists who threw in their efforts with the war. He held true to his convictions and expected to be sent to prison. What he would have said of this last war I do not know. He seemed to me at that time to represent the most sterling virtues of the best English tradition – a stubborn integrity armed against every bribe, a moral courage nobly indifferent to the opinion of others, and a compassionate conscience that led him to devote all his time to the often bitter task of enlightening his fellow men.

Jeannette and Homer were now living in the country, where I went to visit them. My head was full of politics at this time, and I read two newspapers daily, missing not a word of the Parliamentary debates. Jeannette, being necessarily entangled in her household affairs, and having a mind wisely remote from the ephemeral contentions of political controversy, must have found my conversation often boring, but instead of blaming me she blamed herself, saying in an apologetic tone, "I really must read the papers more," which at scattered moments she endeavored to do. She always came away with some strange incident, such as the escape of a python from the zoo, the death of an elephant from grief at the loss of his mate, or the removal of a living man from the stomach of an alligator; and to this day my mind reverts to those singular occurrences, whereas I have long since ceased to remember the words of defunct politicians who presided over the Council Chambers of State in those stormy hours.

My nephew Homer was now old enough to be taken for walks. He was a grave, imaginative little boy who could never, all through his childhood, bear any sight of cruelty towards animals. We used to go to a round pond that mirrored the clouds in the sky. He shared my pleasure in watching the wayward habits of ducks and would stand contemplating them for almost as long as Proust stood before the May tree. I wanted to be something more to him than an aunt – a person, a friend. I hope I succeeded, for he charmed me as few children ever have.

My sister asked me to take my niece, aged four, back to America with me to visit her grandparents. We sailed on the *Mauretania* in early spring.

We had a stateroom shared by three other occupants. My niece slept under me and woke very early in the morning, when she would begin singing little songs to herself. This disturbed the other passengers, so I told her she must lie very still until it was time to get up. The next morning, at the hour when her songs usually began, I felt something prodding my spine and, leaning over the side of my berth, I saw my niece lying with a foot raised like a ballet dancer's so that the tip of her toe could just achieve its cunning intention. I was on the point of reprimanding her with some heat when I saw on her face an expression of such ineffable sweetness and lively good spirits that I withheld my words; and every morning at the same hour this little drama would be repeated. I realized, as never before, the difficulties of children in an arbitrary, grown-up world, with no spokesman to present their case.

Being of an adventurous nature, my niece would want to explore some of the fascinating mysteries about her and not stay still as a daisy in a paddock. Once I discovered her two decks below with one of the sailors. With the exasperation we are apt to feel towards someone we love who has caused us anxiety, I scolded her roundly, and I saw in her face an expression of banked-up rebellion and mute hopelessness that reminded me of myself.

We arrived safely in port, though there had been a number of alarms. Once the engines were reversed and the ship brought to a vibrating, shuddering standstill. Stewards raced up and down the passages, and we could hear the creaking of ropes and the sound of lifeboats being lowered. For one second I felt deep in my marrow what it would be like to be plunged, with all my senses aflame, into the powerful sea.

Chapter XIX

DISAPPOINTMENT IN RETROSPECT

I HAD made up my mind to support myself in New York. Cornelia had found a furnished room for me in Patchin Place, just around the corner from her. It was on a ground floor and was rented to me by a woman as thin as a spill, with a sharp, emaciated countenance and a tongue that took its long-needed repose only in slumber. She lived with an old man, supposedly her husband, though she confided to me that their "union" had never been "consecrated."

Clyde was my first visitor. He invited me to go to a fancy dress ball. He mentioned that Gareth would be there, and it was for this reason that I took so much care with my costume.

It was not until I had danced with several partners that I caught a glimpse of him waltzing with a girl. He looked startled and confused, but we were whirled apart, and he never sought me out to ask me to dance.

I was so struck down that I hardly heard what Clyde was saying as we drove back in a taxi to Patchin Place. "May I come in a moment?" he asked in a peculiar tone after he had dismissed the taxi. It was four o'clock in the morning.

Our relationship had always been what might be called a reliable one – if any relationship may be called that. We were comrades in arms, spokesmen for the downtrodden. It was in this clear upper air of firm purpose and honest hearts that we had our meetings. When we waltzed together, or went to the theatre together, it was still in a spirit of simple fellowship, gay but not giddy, warm but easy. With Maurice I felt behind his words always the possibility of passion, and with Gareth there were so many crooked paths, so much that beckoned and so much that evaded that I had but to summon his image before me to be tormented.

Now, when Clyde asked me his unusual question in his unusual tone, I was in full retreat, thinking only of being by myself so that I could recover from my bitter disappointment. "I'm afraid we might wake up the Butlers."

He hesitated, looking down uncertainly. "Well, good-by," he said at last.

"Good-by," I answered, "and thank you for giving me such a lovely time."

It was certainly odd asking to come into my room at four o'clock in the morning, but most of all odd for Clyde to do so.

A few days after the dance, Gareth called to see me. He was going to Boston to live and had come to bid me good-by. I was still disturbingly attracted to him. He did not stay for long.

Many years later, after I was married, I had to go to Boston to visit a friend who was ill. As I was advancing towards the station platform to catch my train back to New York, I came face to face with Gareth Channing. We stopped and shook hands.

"So you still live in Boston?" I asked. "I suppose you're married."

"Yes, are you?"

"Yes. Are you happy?" I continued.

"Oh, yes, but I've not been married long. Are *you* happy?"

I laughed. "I've been married a long time, or at least a long time for marriage."

"And are you happy?"

"Yes."

"Well, that's a good thing, we're both married and both happy. Can't we go somewhere and have some refreshments?"

"I'm afraid I haven't time before my train leaves." Then, with that recklessness we are apt to feel when we think we shall never see a person again I added, "You knew I was in love with you?"

"Can't you possibly take another train back? Otherwise you should never have said that."

"Well, aren't we both married and both happy, and does it matter what I say now?"

He looked utterly disconcerted. "You bewildered me before, you bewilder me now."

"That's one way in which we're alike. We each bewilder the other."

"But I'm so simple."

"The train is coming. I must hurry."

"You always evade me. I was afraid."

"Afraid!" I laughed derisively. "Afraid of what?"

The train was now pulling up at the station platform. Some passengers pushed between us and prevented his answering, and by the time we could join each other again I had to mount the steps of the train.

"Tell me your married name, how I can reach you."

"I haven't changed it," and then I added lightly, as the signal was given for the train to start, "I've changed nothing." These were the last words to pass between us.

Chapter XX

RANDOLPH BOURNE

My room with its homely backyard onto which my window opened delighted me, but I had to earn my living, and anxiety ate into all my pleasures.

Cornelia advised me to see Miss Joanna Prince, who was the director of a school for socialism. She offered me a position at ten dollars a week with my afternoons free. This was barely enough to live on, but I was promised more lucrative work later.

Miss Prince was tall, with a Junoesque figure, waving blue-black hair, and eyes full of friendly intelligence. She was a woman of large sympathies and balanced judgment who had spent a year in England working with the Fabian Society. After the success of the Russian revolution she went to Russia and was given a post with the Soviet government. She showed some disaffection, and, returning home, was engaged in writing a book when, on her way to her office one morning, she mysteriously disappeared. The manuscript sheets of her book had gone from her desk at the same time. She has never been heard of since.

Randolph Bourne

Randolph Bourne was waiting for me when I returned from my first morning's work. He made everything seem diverting. His mind played around every person, every incident. His wit was directed particularly against the "intellectuals" – the professors, sober and sententious, administering with dry smiles dry sips of dead cultures to young men and women bewildered by their own coursing blood and their own wild and incommunicable thoughts.

But perhaps all society would fly up into the air were it not pinned down by these mumbling pedants. He who is not a strong swimmer had best float with the current.

There was a young man just coming into notice, Walter Lippman, who never failed to stir Randolph's invention, perhaps because he admired him so much. I remember their debating in my rooms the question of America entering the war. Randolph's mind was so acute and informed, so ready to spring from every direction, so "plastic and inflammable," and at the same time so lucid and logical that all were nervous of disagreeing with him. He was never more resourceful than when under fire. Though he was to so large an extent the leader of his generation in education and politics, his chief interest centered upon personal relationships. He was one of the few people I have known who could combine interest in causes with a subtle perception, "perception kept at the pitch of passion." He had an inspired, almost Proustian gift for uncovering the motives of human conduct. Nothing was too small or too great to serve him as quarry. His mind moved in every direction, was porous to every atmosphere.

His odd appearance – one of his ears was conspicuously malformed – had the effect of attracting to him only people of ardor and sincerity. I remember Scofield Thayer saying to me that he thought him very distinguished in appearance and was always proud to be seen with him. He wore a long black student's cape and a black felt hat, and his small, humped figure was a familiar sight in Greenwich Village. People would turn to stare after him with the expression that any deviation from the normal seems inevitably to evoke among the vulgar. It was rather like the expression I had seen in the eyes of the company at Mme. Rôze's when Mr. Parsons had a choking fit.

His most steadfast friends were two attractive young women with whom he used to remain for long periods both in the country and in the city. Agnes de Lima, with her dark eyes, her infectious laugh, Spanish vivacity, and heart as deep as the sea, shed about the last two years of his life the feeling of security he had always longed for. At the time of which I am writing he had moved to some rooms on Charles Street just round the corner from Patchin Place. We usually dined together, sometimes in my rooms, sometimes at a cheap restaurant called Gallup's, frequented by poor artists and writers. I would often drop in to see him late in the evening and discover a circle of young girls sitting in rapt stillness while he played exquisitely on the piano. Brahms was at that time his favorite composer.

The garment workers had gone out on strike, sixty thousand of them, and I was sent to get stories from them. I would go up the dark stairs of some tenement house and enter a room bare of furniture. Even the woman's wedding ring had been pawned or sold. These women, with their pallid cheeks and haunted eyes, would tell of the searing poverty of their days. Some of the children were stark naked, many close to starvation. I would step once more onto Fifth Avenue, where I would encounter the prosperous crowds lingering before the large plate glass show windows, and I would feel as if the silks and satins, the ingenious adornments and *objets d'art*, contrived to entice a jaded taste, were a thin façade behind which guiltless prisoners were left to perish with nothing said.

My work now consisted in writing stories for the newspapers, picketing, and addressing meetings. The strike lasted for many weeks, and in the end the strikers were starved into a compromise.

This experience convinced me anew of the iniquity and incompetence of the competitive industrial system – costumes selling at large sums to people with large incomes and large wardrobes, while the workers were themselves half starved and half clothed. It was largely because the garment trade was made up exclusively of Jews that the conditions were so bad. Shut up like rats in a cellar, they were paid the lowest wages given to skilled men workers (women do not, of course, count) and bled to the last ounce of their strength. A large percentage of them died of tuberculosis before reaching middle age.

D'Alembert once wrote: "Having learnt by a long mournful experience, not to despise but to mistrust and dread men, I have the courage to love them and the prudence to flee them." But how is it possible for man to flee himself?

When I was earning more money, I would frequently attend the Jewish theatre. It was the best theatre in New York, the most serious, the most artistic, and it had the best actors. I also exchanged Yiddish lessons with a poor Jewish woman for lessons in English. She regarded me at first with suspicion and then with humor. It seemed miraculous to me to find preserved only a few blocks from my very door this poetic and ancient culture. But it would have been well if the Hebrews had brought their Wailing Wall with them. No Jewish community should ever be without a Wailing Wall.

Chapter XXI

A FALSE BEGINNING

SHORTLY after coming to live at Patchin Place I made the painful discovery that Mrs. Butler fancied herself a singer. She told me she had once been on the vaudeville stage. On the first occasion when, without any previous warning, her voice pierced the partition between our two rooms as if it had been so much tissue paper, I caught up my hat and coat and fled. After that, at the first preliminary clearing of Mrs. Butler's throat, accompanied by the chords of the piano, I hurried out into the street.

I would usually walk down to the Battery and return by way of the docks, lingering to watch the lights on the water, or some cargo ship freshly docked.

New York is a romantic city, with its gleaming towers thrust high up into the sky, and its little dark holes of doorways, no bigger than those through which Hänsel and Gretel were lured, dotted along the quayside. Out of these hiding places would suddenly emerge men looking like Old John Silver, or Barlasch of the Guard, or Mazzini – pirates, revolutionaries, simple sailors, some sober, some drunk; bold, free men of all nationalities, with a rolling gait and a roving eye, and their caps on the backs of their heads, and their hands in the pockets of their jackets. I would sometimes see an old man with a countenance as wrinkled as an elephant's hide, and with gold hoops in his ears. My campaigning days had made me careless of danger.

Patchin Place lies under the shadow of the old Jefferson Court, with its sham Gothic tower, where a great clock points out the hours to damned and saved alike. On the upper floor of the building were cells where prisoners were detained until their cases could be allocated to other courts.

Facing the side entrance of the courthouse was a row of lawyers' offices, occupied mostly by Jews. These lawyers would employ detectives to follow girls in the street seeking to solicit them. If the girls showed any signs of response, the detective would immediately put them under arrest. He would then march them up to the office of one of these lawyers, who would promise to dispose of their case on the guarantee of a future payment. The girls, usually penniless, would sign anything to get their freedom and would be saddled with a debt, remorselessly exacted, that might take them years to pay off. Later this iniquitous practice was discovered and put a stop to; but when I first came to live at Patchin Place, hardly a day passed that I did not see some girl, half mad with fright, being decoyed into the toils of these astute men like a fly into a spider's net.

The whole aspect of life revealed by so close a proximity to this court was being continually brought home to me. As I would be returning from work, I would frequently see the Black Maria drive up and its occupants jostled out and herded up the steps like so many sheep being prodded into their pens. There was always an inquisitive knot of people standing to watch them, and I, too, would look into the faces of these unlucky ones – lucky rogues gazing at unlucky rogues; for, as Hazlitt once said: "Many a man would have turned rogue if he had known how." I remember one girl with a childish countenance to whom I tried to communicate a feeling of sympathy; but she gazed at me with wide, staring eyes – as I have seen a rabbit look at a stoat.

Sometimes I would hear women calling out from their cells. On one occasion a woman howled half through the night. I could hear her as I lay stiff in my bed, this howl of a trapped human animal, rising to a shriek of frenzy and subsiding to a low wail of unutterable terror and despair. The sound became finally intolerable to me, and I dressed and went over to the night policeman. I begged him to send someone up to pacify the woman or to allow me to go up to her. "Oh, don't you think nothing about that, Miss," he said in a fatherly way. "She'll come round in the morning. They often takes on like that." Human woes were all shoved along like so many packages in the post office. Nobody noticed, nobody cared.

On the floor above me lived an Englishwoman, secretary to Isadora Duncan, who was as sensitive to noises as I. In a courtyard facing our windows, an Alsatian wolfhound was fastened up at night, and his baying would often prevent us from sleeping. Once she tapped on my door at five o'clock in the morning, asking if I would come with her to complain to the owner. Fortified and enlivened by desperation, we marched boldly up to his door. The man yelped out oaths that must have wakened the inhabitants of all the adjacent houses. The only people abroad at this hour were milkmen. I liked to hear the clip-clop of the horses' hoofs, followed by the rattle of the milk bottles. It is a sound that gives reassurance – as if broken vows and trapped girls are not the whole of life.

A great city by light of dawn seems to be purged of sordidness, washed clean like the decks of a ship. I did not go back to my bed, but walked over to the west side docks and watched a houseboat anchored a little way out. There was a young man in charge of it, and presently he came ashore. He was tall, fair, and slim, and his eyes were the color of a child's blue satin party sash. He was Swedish, and his name was Sven. He said he was lonely, and I told him he might come to see me.

I heard many stories from this ingenuous young man, who had run away to sea as a boy. He had been in every kind of ship and served in every kind of capacity. He was an expert chef and cooked me delicious dinners. His sister was a famous cinema star, but he was too proud to communicate with her. He always carried his money in his shoe. Though he looked as mild as white clover, he frequently got into street brawls. He had contracted syphilis in a port in France and had only recently been released from the hospital where he had been receiving treatment. He soon went off in his boat, but for many years he would appear suddenly at my door, with the look of salt wind in his hair and with fresh adventures to recount and some trinket, wrapped about in an old piece of tarpaulin, that he would pull out of an inside pocket and shyly hand to me.

Among my feminine acquaintance was a young woman named Stephanie, whose chic appearance formed a contrast to that of most of the inhabitants of the row. She had as much aplomb as a master tattooist. She had been managing editor of a newspaper, but a man had been put in her place and she was now out of work. She was going out on a tugboat to write up her experiences for the magazine section of a popular newspaper and she asked me to accompany her. She was always urging me to write, insisting that nothing was easier than to earn one's living with one's pen. "All you have to do is to put down what you see, make up what you don't see, and keep it lively. Try it, for I know you're a born writer."

We took a streetcar to the Battery and were rowed out to the tugboat, where the crew were expecting us. The sea was flecked with surf, and there was a fresh breeze blowing. We conducted a large, ocean-going steamer into harbor by means of a long rope attached from the stern of our boat to the prow of the steamer. The men gave us scalding hot coffee and rolls in the galley while they entertained us with stories of their adventures.

The following evening, with my window open upon the backyard, and Mrs. Butler miraculously silent, I sat down before my table with pen and paper and an anxious determination to write up this happy experience.

I could see it all clearly before my eyes, the sparkling blue waters, the boat with its black funnel, the name *Minnie* painted in red letters, the stokehole, the bunkers, the galley, the men's quarter. I could remember the look of every man and even the names they called one another. Yet the vivid experience of those hours evaded words as a colt evades the halter. I stared at the virgin sheet of paper "defended by its own whiteness," then I rose and looked out of the window at a cat stepping nimbly along the fence and thought how free a life a cat's was. Once more I seated myself and dipped my pen in the ink – which got drier and drier on the nib as I held it poised over the page.

At last I gave it all up and decided that any life was preferable to that of a writer – all hope and no fulfillment. I had written stories about the garment workers for the papers, but this was because I was deeply stirred, and I had written articles in my suffrage days, but this was because I was writing for a cause I had closely at heart. I was evidently a propagandist writer only.

Had I known then the experiences of many illustrious authors, I might have been emboldened to cling to my pen with a little firmer grasp, or to return to the attack with a stouter heart. "I sit down to my work with despair and rise from it with sorrow," Balzac makes one of his characters say. Hazlitt describes an early effort of his at composition in the following manner: "I got pen and paper, determined to make clear work of it, wrote a few meager sentences in the style of a mathematical demonstration, stopped half way down the second page; and after trying in vain to pump up any words, images, notions, apprehensions, facts, or observations . . . gave up the attempt as labor in vain, and shed tears of helpless despondency on the blank unfinished page."

I awaited with interest Stephanie's article, which finally appeared with a sketch of the boat and a photograph of the skipper. It was sensational and informative, with comic touches. Everything was described differently from the way I should have described it. I decided with a sad finality that I should never be able to make my living by my pen.

Chapter XXII

MILLIGAN PLACE AND NEW FRIENDS

My mother had been staying for some time in Colorado Springs, where my brother had gone for his health. My father received a telegram saying that my brother was critically ill, and he asked me to go out to her. I gave up my position and left in two days' time. I had never fully absorbed the seriousness of my brother's illness. He had recovered on so many occasions that I thought he would do so now, and the novelty of being swept through immense prairies, of watching the sun – like a huge balloon – disappear behind this vast yellow landscape drove all thought from my mind. One grows accustomed to the vastness of the ocean, but to look out upon measureless acres of land, untrodden by human foot, brings home in a new and startling manner the magnitude of the planet.

At the sight of my brother's face, love and pity flooded my heart. Never before had I so clearly realized the tragic struggle of his days. He had come safely through the crisis, but was still too weak to raise himself in bed.

The air was intoxicating, and now that the immediate threat to my brother's life had passed, my mother was anxious that I should see something of the country and meet her friends. The society was divided between those that were there to study at the university, and those that were there for their health. It was a center of cosmopolitan culture and earnest pursuit of knowledge; and the mountains, with their glens and lakes and picturesque canyons, were a perpetual temptation to explore.

I used sometimes to attend lectures at the university and heard Rabindranath Tagore speak on one of these occasions. His voice was like wind blowing through a hollow reed. He seemed to belong to an entirely different species from that of the youth who were seeking so intently to unravel the meaning wrapped in his quavering message.

I spent five weeks in Colorado Springs, most of the time pursuing my own pleasures. Occasionally I would read to my brother and I would sit with him after his nurse had washed him in the morning. I never saw him show any sign of weakness, nor did I hear a complaint pass his lips. I caught in his eyes at rare moments a look of stoical sadness, but, as a rule, they were full of light. In our latter years, mists clear from our minds, and our actions are seen in their more enduring aspects. Since my mother never betrayed her anguish, I remained ignorant of what she was feeling. I always consider as one of the serious failures of my life my lack of imaginative insight into her heart and into my brother's during this time.

Cornelia had rented for me, in my absence, the top floor of the house in which she was living in Milligan Place. My mother had given me some furniture, and Randolph had been using the rooms until my arrival.

I now had to make haste to find some means of earning my living. Most of the women I knew were writers or social workers, or they were pursuing some precarious artistic enterprise. Sometimes they had full purses; then, for weeks they would go hungry, those that were up sharing with those that were down. Women had to live by their wits – not their wit, that was best kept out of sight – their good nature, and their personal appearance, otherwise drudgery and low wages were their portion. They could force their way into the professions only against obstacles that prevented all but the most determined and brilliant from keeping up the struggle. And from where were they to get the money for their training?

No sooner was I fully settled in my rooms than melancholy fell upon me. This was due largely to anxiety about the future and it made me realize the importance of a sense of security in the lives of working people.

At Cornelia's suggestion I went to call on an acquaintance of hers who was about to start a league to promote a new form of education, and I was at once engaged.

Stella Fane was an attractive woman, with a slender figure, rebellious hair, generous eyes, and a mouth as determined as a pope's. I shall not go, here, into an explanation of the system of education she was advancing. It had originated in Gary, Indiana, and a public school of sixteen hundred children in the Bronx, New York, had adopted it. These schools had aroused interest among educators all over the world, one of them being Mme. Montessori, whom I had taken to visit the school in the Bronx.

Since to alter the educational system of a great city involved a large expenditure of public money, we found the Tammany machine working against us. Never had I met more violent and more unprincipled opposition. Mrs. Fane was a born fighter. The greater the opposition, the more she rose to meet it. She had at heart the welfare of the children, and this, combined with her indomitable and fiery will, kept her as resolute as Frederick the Great and as impassioned as Garibaldi.

I was given a position as organizer, with a car to drive and two girls to work with me. Our speakers were usually mothers of school children, university professors, and prominent philanthropists. The schools were a burning issue, and we would have been mobbed frequently, had it not been for the police.

Stella Fane's husband was an ultra-refined Englishman, with an Oxford accent and artistic tastes. He would sometimes object plaintively to her activities, but she would rush into their flat, her arms laden with packages, just in time to cook him a meal not to be surpassed by Felix, the head chef of the Ritz. Then she would wash up the dishes in less time than it takes a good Catholic to say his beads, and be off again.

She took her pleasures as she took her work, at high speed. She dressed for battle, as had Madame, but with a final touch of seduction, for she was susceptible to men, and they were attracted by her. She was always too kind to me, covering up my deficiencies and praising my scanty talents.

My work was not, however, my real life. It drove me forward through the days, anxious, excited, responsible, and weary. The pursuit of "truth," the cultivation of friendship, and the rewards of solitude, these were my real life.

At Milligan Place I had now what might be called a circle, or rather several circles, none of which touched. Among my friends was a young man called Brian, who looked rather like a German student. He had a mass of unruly auburn hair, and nearsighted eyes, and he always carried some large book under his arm. Randolph thought him pedantic, but with each friend we create a world shut off from our other friends. It was his mind that attracted me to him. He, too, was pursuing "truth," and all his search was the outcome of an impassioned nature. There was nothing on which he did not shed light – conscience, religion, love, free will – all those subjects that have, since the earliest times, engaged the thoughts of philosophers.

We would sit half through the night in front of my glowing coals, and the preoccupations of my feverish days would give place to "divine philosophy"; for "the happy man is one who is freed from both fear and desire because of the gift of reason."

Brian lived with two friends in a poor section of the city. One of them, Otto, was a professional cellist of eccentric habits. Like Swinburne, when he made Rosetti so uneasy, he liked running through their flat stark naked. The other one, Robin, was a fair young man, with so highly developed a sense of the comic that he was kept in perpetual shouts over the oddities of his two companions. He picked up a living as best he could, borrowing the Sunday suit of his Italian grocer, who was flattered at his request, to hunt for a job, and looking in it as conventional and crafty as a successful lawyer.

Among the friends I shared with Randolph was a cultured young man called Paul Rosenfeld. I remember my surprise when Randolph first took me to his rooms for dinner. He lived as a bachelor, but in this gracious interior, with its Viennese atmosphere, it was as if the rustling of skirts still lingered. Most of our lives are passed with other people, yet human intercourse is rarely regarded as an art. Paul Rosenfeld was one who treated it as such – without vanity or competition: "*la fantasie qu'exigent les humanités*." He preserved by some rare quality the social tone. He was versatile in all the arts but was known most widely as a musical critic, and no composer or musician of note came to New York without receiving entertainment from him. On warm evenings he would fetch me to drive with him in an open victoria or a hansom cab – a few of these vehicles were still to be hired – while discoursing all the time on the value of the passing moment that alone existed:

> I dreamèd fast of mirth and play,
> In youth is pleasure. In youth is pleasure.

We would have a *café mousse* or a *parfait framboise* at some open air pavilion in the park, and I would return to my rooms, my head giddy with the strains of "*Valse Octobre*" or "*Love's Golden Dream.*"

In the rooms under me lived 'Big Jim Larkin,' the famous leader of the Dublin dock strikers. He was an enormous man with a shock of iron-gray hair and a face lined with resolution and anxiety. He was the most intractable of revolutionaries and was heading a movement of the most exploited and poorly paid workers, those excluded from the orthodox trade unions, and he was under close supervision by the police. Later he was tried and sent to prison. He had more imagination than any labor leader I have ever met, and my sympathies were all with him. It seemed to me a most shameful thing to send so good a man to prison while the streets were swarming with so many wicked ones.

Mrs. Magowan, the janitress of our alley, was a little Irish woman with bones as light as a bird's. She always wore a large, dusty bow of black satin ribbon on her small, gray head. The greater part of her day she spent bowed over the ash and refuse bins sorting out their contents. When she was sober she had a certain deportment, but when she was drunk her voice would carry almost as far as Mrs. Butler's, nor was its burden any languishing love ditty, but good round oaths that had seen service over a lifetime and had lost none of their trenchancy for all that. She had been a lady's maid for some celebrated millionaire families and described her impressions of her employers in terms such as Swift might have envied. Like Mary Wollstonecraft, she had decided that independence was the basis of all virtue.

Near the entrance of Milligan Place was a small cigar shop. The proprietor, Mr. Smith, was a large man of a genial temperament and used, whenever I passed him, to boom out in his deep bass voice: "You're my girl. You're the belle of Sixth Avenue." On summer evenings there would be a group of idle old men in front of his shop, tipped back in chairs, nodding their heads, and narrowly scrutinizing everyone who went in and out of the alley. In winter they would be pressed close together before the small stove that heated his shop, still in a perpetual *bavardage*.

A tiny flower shop was at the other side of the entrance. The proprietress was a beautiful young Irish woman, whose husband had left her with three infants to support. She used to hang a basket of flowers on one arm and, with a baby in her free one, and the others clinging to her skirts, she would go from restaurant to restaurant. Even in the coldest weather she appeared lighthearted and would seem, standing among her bright-colored flowers in her chilly alcove, like a kind of Flora transported from the sunny mountains of Hymettus.

A woman, called Mrs. Carroll, came each morning to wash my dishes and tidy my rooms for me. She was delicately built, with a mass of fine-spun, prematurely gray hair over a pinched countenance from which two large, liquid eyes regarded one with a tired and unaccusing anxiety. She, too, had been left with a family of little children to bring up, and was just able to keep starvation at bay. Wherever one looked there seemed to be women scrubbing floors, taking in washing, scouring greasy pots in sordid underground kitchens – humble women, bowed down under the burden of the days, yet seldom voicing a complaint. I once heard two eminent English psychologists gravely debating whether women had the physical strength to fill the position of a foreign diplomat – a recollection that has always amused me.

Chapter XXIII

AN ENCOUNTER

When America came into the war in April, 1917, my friends were, with few exceptions, pacifists. Randolph wrote an article which was published in a magazine given up ostensibly to the arts. The patrons withdrew their support and the magazine was forced to cease publication. He had never had any trouble in placing his work, but now every editor's door was closed against him. I remember his ironical amusement when a man who had been receiving a salary at Columbia University for the sole purpose of preaching pacifism among the students was stealthily disposed of the moment there was any real threat of war. Americans of my generation had been brought up to regard war as a disgrace to any country. The Woman's Peace Party had organized a parade longer than any of our great suffrage parades.

My rooms were for a time a center for stormy discussions. Randolph would keep bringing new acquaintances with him – journalists, artists, young revolutionaries, university professors – some of them lately arrived from Europe. He was for his generation in America, in the matter of the war, what Bertrand Russell was for his in England and Romain Rolland for his in France.

Among all the people I saw at that time, I can recall only a few who had any enthusiasm over the war. Yet the papers supported it, the socialists fell into line, and what had been a little whirlpool of contention and resistance became one vast surging river of hysterical action. Randolph always held that as soon as America entered the war she lost her bargaining power as a great nation, and that before joining with France and England she should make known to the world her peace aims.

Cornelia had an East Indian friend, who came sometimes to call on her, and she was suspected of shielding some East Indian rebels. Her rooms were searched and a detective employed to watch everyone going in and coming out of our alley. He was a plump, conventionally dressed man, with blond hair plastered tight to his skull and a smooth, inscrutable countenance. His shoes were as pointed as those of my old dancing master, perhaps in order to push their way through cracks. It was my friend, Mr. Smith, who whispered the secret to me. Cornelia laughed, and always referred to him as "my detective." He became as familiar to us as the ashcan cats. Most of my friends fell under suspicion, and Randolph, who combined an irrepressible imprudence with a supercautious alarm, went to stay with his friend Van Wyck Brooks in the country. We had some argument, just before he left that prompted me in a moment of injudicious playfulness to send him a telegram containing the one word: PERFIDE. This was a cause of extreme agitation to him, as it was suspected by the postal authorities – whose knowledge of French was as scanty as their wits were slow and their heads hot – of being a code word. He had the greatest difficulty in quieting their suspicions.

My work with Stella came to an end in the early summer, and I obtained through her a position with an Americanization study, financed by the Carnegie Foundation. There were in

America two opposed schools of opinion in regard to the foreign populations. One wished to assimilate them into American institutions. The other wished to preserve their differences and help them to continue the arts and crafts of their home lands. It was to this latter group that the study with which I was about to be engaged belonged.

I had two weeks' vacation, and leisure was so delicious to me that I did not wish to squander a moment. Merely to know that I could rise when I liked, walk nonchalantly out in the morning sunshine, linger over the fruit stalls, read in my room, and let my thoughts come up from their secret hiding places, was happiness enough. Not squandering my time meant for me recapturing my sense of awareness, our most priceless gift, and the one most precariously balanced. To be sure, there was the anxiety that always accompanied a change of work. It was, however, like knowing on a journey that one is approaching a dark tunnel, but in the meantime delighting in the scenes from the train window.

On my first free Sunday I decided I would have my breakfast at the Brevoort Hotel, where it was the custom for Greenwich Village literati to gather for coffee and *croissants* and the best French butter.

I took my seat in the corner of the dining room, and presently a man I knew slightly – he had spoken during the garment strike at some of our meetings – placed himself with his companion at a nearby table. His back was turned to me, but his friend sat facing me and our glances would occasionally meet. He was tall and dark, with a great deal of black hair brushed back from a high forehead. He had a bold nose, sensual lips, and large Spanish eyes, reflective and guarded.

The waiter was long in bringing my bill, and by the time I had received my change, they too were preparing to leave. I bowed to my acquaintance, Professor Bartlett, and, descending the outdoor steps, was about to walk away, when the two men overtook me. Professor Bartlett introduced his companion as M. Renault, then, as a Fifth Avenue bus came into sight, he signaled it to stop and, with a hasty farewell, left us together.

"May I walk with you? Where you are going?" M. Renault said uncertainly.

"I wasn't really going anywhere."

"That will suit me perfectly," he laughed. He spoke with a slight foreign accent.

We passed through Washington Arch and entered the little square. It was a lovely summer morning without a cloud in the sky, and children were tumbling in the grass and rolling their hoops along the sidewalks. We seated ourselves on one of the benches.

"I can tell you've lived on the continent," he said.

"How can you?"

"It's difficult to say, but I'm sure I'm not mistaken."

He accompanied me back to Milligan Place and seemed loath to leave me. "May I take you out for dinner this evening?" he asked.

Soon I was in love, drawn deeper and deeper into a peculiar delirium that made all my daily life seem unreal and only those moments when I was in my lover's arms, of value.

Pierre Renault would come to my rooms in the late afternoon, and after our love-making we would go out into the deserted streets, and wtih the last rays of the setting sun turning the horizon into brilliant golds and yellows, and night coming on, a clinging desolation would pervade me. We would sit opposite one another in some restaurant, and he would seem entirely foreign to me; and this would cause me, with a convulsive anxiety, to seek to bridge the distance between us until once more I could lose myself in this love.

Pierre's mother was a Spanish Jewess, and his father a French Gentile. He had published some books of a semi-sociological order and had been sent by the French government to America to make certain *rapprochements*. He was both ambitious and unimplicated, with the melancholy fatalism inherited from his mother, and the febrile brilliance that his Parisian upbringing had given him.

We seldom discussed ideas. Our relationship was charged with a deeper mystery than that of brittle thought. He was musical and would sing old Hebrew melodies in a way that evoked far-off centuries and eternal joys and sorrows. We would come back from dinner, and he would spend the night with me, and in the morning we would have our coffee and rolls in my room, with the sun lying across the table, and the scent of the flowers he had brought me conjuring our senses. Sometimes we would go out to the French pastry shop for our breakfast, where other clandestine lovers were looking furtively round to see if they were being noticed.

Even my work did not cause me the anxiety I would have felt if my life had not been centered upon this secret love. My new offices, on upper Fifth Avenue, were the most luxurious I had been in. The people engaged in the study were all university professors, experienced research students, or distinguished representatives of the various nationalities we were about to consider – among them the late Professor Mazaryk, president of Czechoslovakia.

The first thing I was asked to do was to visit the offices of the Italian newspapers and look through their old files for references to the *Mafia* and the *Camorra*, secret criminal societies, introduced into the United States by men from Sicily and Naples, who were often freshly released from prison sentences in their own country. The editor of the *Bolletino della Sera* was most gracious and gave me a room to myself in which to work, and enough newspapers to employ, I should have thought, a whole staff of assiduous workers for the rest of their days. Soon I was caught up in such a succession of dire and dramatic occurrences that I was swept forward from journal to journal as a hound follows the scent of a fox. I have never been a reader of detective stories, but these events were lifted hot from life. It was an occupation that would have delighted De Quincey. There was a famous Italian detective named Petrosino, very like Sherlock Holmes, who at last trailed two of the worst criminals back to Italy, where he was stabbed in the spine as he was about to have them put under arrest. I spent all my mornings for several weeks in this office.

The staff of the study would sometimes dine together in a foreign section of the city. At one of these dinners, in a Russian restaurant, we all sat round the table sipping vodka and breaking up thick slices of black bread, while one of the professors, a man with a beetling brow and the shoulders of a Hercules, talked in measured tones about "fringe cases." He had written several books on the Negroes.

I have, as a rule, found sociologists and historians more interesting than scientists, their studies involving them in a knowledge of human life and the drama of human existence. Scientists can sometimes seem as unobservant of the teeming world about them as a busy embryo. Not that I have any intention of criticizing these highly endowed men who so unselfishly devote their brief hours to cutting into healthy animals in order to experiment with sick ones, and to discovering new and ingenious ways of obliterating whole mild populations. Like the baker who turns out hot sugared buns and is not supposed to concern himself with the digestion of his customers, so scientists are not supposed to concern themselves with the results of their remarkable discoveries. Their fidelity is to "the isolated fact," and if they inadvertently put an end to the entire human race, they will, it cannot be doubted, themselves die valiantly, their microscopes glued as tight to their eyes as limpets to rocks. Or are they the greatest of all the great benefactors of humanity and determined upon speeding along that universal impulse towards death and destruction which, as Freud has suggested, is the underlying motive of human existence?

Chapter XXIV

ENCHANTMENT

THOUGH I could frequently banish Pierre from my thoughts, I carried my knowledge of him always in my bones. He was my "glassy essence." I would sometimes wait for him in his rooms. They were up three flights of stairs, and I would step cautiously lest I meet his landlady. We had each a latchkey to the other's door. When I spent the night with him I would steal away very early in the morning. I would feel in the familiar streets, now so empty, as if my love were something I had imagined, and yet that it was the only reality of my days. It robbed me of everything but itself, and yet it receded from me.

In my room matters were easier. Old Mrs. Magowan was occupied exclusively with her alley bins. They were to her the round globe and all that it contained – and to Mrs. Carroll, anything I did would have seemed proper and right. As for society, it condones what it is allowed to ignore. The most atrocious crimes – rape of little children, incest, murder – all may flourish, provided the smooth outer surface shows no conspicuous rent. I have seen two policemen exchange humorous glances when a woman shouted frantically for help from the upper story of a house because her husband was beating her. When I ventured to offer a remonstrance their reply was that they never interfered between a man and his wife.

I would occasionally go home for week ends to my parents. My brother had died some months after I left Colorado Springs, and my mother had returned with a wound in her heart which nothing ever healed. She always gave grace to my homecoming. I hinted to her that I had a "friend" and she accepted the implication as she accepted all the divergencies from her group. She did not mind, as long as I was happy and discreet. I would come back to New York and take a car through the empty Sunday afternoon streets, and my heart would beat faster and faster as I came nearer and nearer to Milligan Place. Sometimes I would find Pierre waiting for me, sometimes I would be the first to arrive; and my senses would be on fire listening for the opening of the outer door and the sound of his quick steps coming up the stair.

One Sunday, we went on an expedition to Long Beach, taking our lunches with us. We walked along the packed yellow sand with the salt wind blowing in our faces. The waves, one fast upon the other, rose to their white crests, glittered like green, transparent glass, and dashed themselves out, the foam sucking up close to our feet and receding in long streamers. I was conscious of some lack of accord between us, too vague to define, something that made him more than ever eager to please me.

The train was crowded, when we returned that night, with tired mothers and restless children, and I experienced one of those moments when he became for me an utter stranger. This was an anomaly of love, apparently. It was everything or it was nothing. As human beings, we hardly knew each other, as lovers, we touched secrets that broke down every barrier. For those moments either of us would have thrown away the rest of our days as lightly as one blows out a candle.

I had a friend, Linda, a tall, impetuous, attractive girl. She knew of Pierre's and my love, and when, in the early autumn, she heard that he was to leave New York for a week end, she persuaded me to go with her to a mountain village during his absence. As a rule I would have loved such a holiday, but now I could think only with regret that my lover was not there to share it with me, and I realized for the first time that he might at any moment be returning to Paris. I had never contemplated marriage and I did not do so now, yet everything outside my love was a drop into the void.

After Linda had gone to bed, I lay on the hot feather mattress, unable to sleep. Finally I got up and dressed. Stepping softly into the damp night, I walked along the narrow dirt road. The stars were obscured by clouds, and I could barely make out the path ahead of me. Mystery was everywhere. I felt it in my bones, in the cry of the katydids that pierced the midnight stillness. And around this mystery were lonely spaces in a universe without meaning and without bottom. Only in love was there forgetfulness, because in love the mystery did not turn against us. I made up my mind that I would pack all my rapture, all my gaiety, all the resources of my spirit, as never before, into the coming hours with Pierre.

He had told me that he would be back on Monday, and when I came to New York on Sunday evening, I felt as if a century of time still separated us. It was late, and I decided that I would bring something to eat to my rooms. Dropping my bag, I went back down the stairs, intending to go to the French delicatessen shop on Sixth Avenue, but I turned the corner at Tenth Street instead and went towards a shop on Greenwich Avenue where Pierre and I had frequently bought caviar. How desolate a city can look when empty of life! Not even a tramway was in sight, or a motor car, or a dog. The blinds were drawn down over all the windows.

As I approached the shop, a man and woman came out of the door and started to walk towards me. They stopped while he took some packages from her arms. The man was Pierre. I fled down a side street and continued to walk blindly through street after street, my steps carrying me instinctively towards the Battery. That one glance I had caught had extinguished my life. He had never gone away. He had never loved me. His kisses were false, his words were false, and love, from beginning to end, was a mockery and a delusion. I wanted one thing only, to be no more.

I made up my mind to drown myself, or rather, some blind force drove me towards this end. I would sometimes brush against men coming out of doorways. They would begin to follow me but would fall back as I went swiftly on. I came to the Battery. The benches were full of couples. Cutting across the park, past the grandstand, I plunged down a narrow street, unconscious of my surroundings.

I do not know how long I walked in this manner, but when I got back to the Battery, the benches were empty and no one was in sight. Always the memory of those two laid waste my life. A thousand images swam into my mind, the most clear being the face of my father. It was as if my mind were a coursing river down which fragments of my past, broken off from any meaning, were constantly being dashed; and the words, "love has gone, love has gone, love has gone," sounded ceaselessly in my ears.

I grasped the top bar of the iron railing that separated me

from the waters below, and as I did so, I was conscious of a step at my side. Startled, I turned round and saw a large man, a sailor with a broad, good-natured countenance, his sailor's cap, round as a silver dollar, tipped over one ear.

"What's the matter, little girl?" he said, "has someone done you dirt? You look fair upset."

"Has anyone ever been false to you?" I asked him.

"Aw gee!" he laughed. "They're all false to me."

"Have you ever been false to anyone?"

"A sailor don't get no time to make up to a girl, so it's easy come, easy go."

"Do you believe in love?"

"Gawd!" he laughed, "I never thought much about it, but if I found the right little girl, I'd serve her honest."

I have always believed that this man, if he did not save my life, saved my reason. He gave me back a sense of proportion. I determined I would shut Pierre out of my thoughts, draw a thick curtain over my memories, yet I knew that this was impossible.

When I left the elevated train at Eleventh Street, I saw the hour hand of the Jefferson Court clock pointing at one. I went through the court and up the stairs, and was just getting out my key when the door was opened from the inside, and Pierre stood before me, his face pale and strained.

"I've been waiting for you since nine o'clock," he said. "Where have you been?"

"But you told me you weren't returning until tomorrow."

"I came back to surprise you."

Perhaps we had never embraced more passionately, but there was a difference in my love. I did not believe him, and in him, too, there was a change. I put it down to his having the other friend. I asked him no questions, but every evening he spent away from me, I suspected him of being with her. I was trying to accustom myself to giving him up. He always cast a spell upon me. I never could touch the depths of his nature. He was barbaric and excessively civilized, gentle and proud, remote and dependent, guarded and spontaneous. He was so strikingly good-looking, so different from all the other men I knew, with his fastidious Latin head and his rich, quick responses that held in them so many reserves and so much – could it be perfidy? But love is, I think, like a moonlit forest, full of false turnings, and with magic lying across it, and all leading to a final darkness. We never saw enough of each other to tire in each other's company. I could be strained and even relieved when he had left me, but we always returned fresh and enthralled to each other's arms. Yet I cannot say that I was happy. What I felt was more like an uneasy enchantment that robbed all the rest of my days of meaning and yet held a menace.

The only thing that could break in upon this spell was the fact that Randolph was ill. I hurried round to see him. He looked strangely pitiful in bed. "I don't want to die," he said, speaking with difficulty; but the words were imbued with his wonted irony, and so deeply involved was I in my love that I could not realize how serious was the threat to his life.

Pierre was waiting in my rooms when I returned late that afternoon, and we decided to have dinner out. As we were turning the corner of Tenth Street, I saw a woman coming towards us and recognized her as the woman who had been with Pierre. She stopped, and I looked into her face. She was unusually plain and past middle age. She shook hands effusively with Pierre, and he introduced me to her.

When we had managed to extricate ourselves, he said, "*C'est une femme bien ennuyeuse*. I'm always running into her. I got caught with her that night I wanted to surprise you. Tell me, *ma petite*, where were you that night?" He had asked me that question before.

He stopped in the middle of the street, with people passing all around us, and in a tone half-serious, half-playful he said, "*Si je croyais que tu m'aies trompé je me tuerais*."

The next afternoon I left my office early. It was late in December, but the sun was shining brightly, and I felt the anticipation of the coming hours stirring my pulse. I made a glowing fire in my grate and then I prepared tea, but when Pierre arrived the tea was forgotten.

It was during our love-making that the telephone began to ring. I thought, at first, I would disregard it, but it became so disturbing that I at last took down the receiver. It was a message to tell me that Randolph had died. I put back the receiver and returned to the arms of my lover. My dearest friend was lying dead on one bed and I was making love on another.

Only after our love-making was over did I plead a headache and ask to be left alone. Pierre looked at me with hurt surprise, but I could not bring myself to tell him of Randolph's death.

I hastened over to my dear friend Agnes, the noblest woman I have known, and learned that Randolph had died as she raised him up in her arms.

Yet it was still my love that absorbed me. What if Pierre did not come back? If he never came back? I went to his rooms, but he was not there. My anxiety gathered force. What if he was angry? I returned to his rooms and left a note, asking him to come to me at once. My clock beat out the seconds, each hammer stroke thrusting deep into my listening nerves.

At last I heard his step. He entered without speaking, seating himself on the edge of a chair as if he did not mean to stay.

"*Vous allez mieux?*" he asked politely.

I burst into tears.

"*Tu m'aimes, tu m'aimes!*" He caught me in his arms.

I went to Randolph's funeral three days later and sat through the service without shedding a single tear, yet I have suffered in the whole of my life but one loss more important to me than the loss of this friend. Our perceptions were miraculously attuned, our quality of humor almost identical. We were stirred by the same indignations, open to the same influences. Living in an age when youth flung itself into causes he had hardly begun to draw upon his most original gifts, as Mr. Van Wyck Brooks has intimated in his beautiful appreciation of him contained in "The History of a Literary Radical," and as his posthumous works would seem to bear out. It was well within his scope to have been America's Jean Jacques Rousseau.

"He is dead. Never shall we hear his voice again, or look into his eyes, or touch his living fingers." Yet each person who has been dear to us changes us in some indefinable manner, and in carrying into the grave so much of our life, leaves with us so much of himself, of what we loved and honored in him, that it is as if in abandoning us he had first inscribed across our spirits an enduring message of consolation.

Chapter XXV

PARTING

PIERRE's and my love of music was a strong bond between us, and when we saw it announced that the Boston Symphony orchestra was to perform Beethoven's Seventh Symphony, we arranged to go to the concert. It was enough for me to see the conductor raise his baton, as a magician takes up his sorcerer's wand, to feel my heart beat more rapidly. It is our sensibility that burns up life, that gives it beauty or robs it of meaning. Music is for me supreme among the arts. Such ravishment cannot be contained in any combination of syllables. It transcends all experience and makes us immortal. It is architectural – a temple reared in space – and it is as insubstantial as arabesques of gossamer that dissolve upon the air. It has within it all the hidden secrets of the psyche, sad and wanton, diabolical and sublime. It carries us up, up, up, higher and ever higher, sweeter and ever sweeter, opening door after door until we are ourselves the mystery it evokes, our spirit turning in unison with the turning of the spheres.

When we got back to Milligan Place I brought out a bottle of Marsala and some biscuits. Pierre was constrained and the music that had seemed to unite us so intimately was as if it had never been. I was always conscious of reserves in him, but they seemed more like riches that I was unable to handle. It was part of the fascination we had, one for the other, that so little was spoken, so much implied. Then suddenly in tones as distinct as the tolling of a bell in mid-ocean, he said: "I'm sailing for France this Friday. My wife has been ill."

"You've taken your berth?" I was at last able to say.

"You're not angry, *ma petite?*"

"Oh, non, non."

"I didn't tell you I was married because at first it didn't seem to matter and then I dreaded to."

"And your wife . . . you're fond of her?"

"Yes."

"And she is faithful?"

"She's some years older than I." He seemed to offer this as an explanation.

"I'm very tired."

"Don't send me away, *ma petite*. What has my wife to do with our love?"

"Would you mind if she had a lover?" He made no answer. "And all the time you've been deceiving us both."

"But I didn't deceive you," he said in desperation.

"And your wife? You didn't deceive her?"

"She doesn't expect me never to make love to another woman."

"And you've . . . ?"

"I've made love only to you."

"I would rather be alone," I said tonelessly.

He took his hat and coat and stood hesitating at the door, then he opened it and I heard his steps go down the stairs and pass into the court. I had known women whose lives had been destroyed because their husbands had left them for younger women, and I had made up my mind that I would never be the cause of suffering to another woman. It was not that I blamed women for striking out for their happiness, or men, either, but I had determined that for my part I would avoid any such situation that might end disastrously.

I pulled off my satin slippers and put on a pair of walking shoes. Flinging on my coat over my evening dress, I turned off the gas and hurried down the stairs. There are occasions when matter drops out of our consciousness, when we are driven forward like leaves in a wind. I found myself going into one of the entrances of Central Park. It was bitterly cold, and the benches were empty. I sat down on one of them. A deadly apathy took possession of me. It all seemed suddenly of no consequence. Love was a madness, and now I was no longer mad. I was awake. I knew what I was doing. At last I got up, my joints stiff with cold. I went through an exit of the park and boarded a Fifth Avenue omnibus that took me to Tenth Street. As I turned the corner at Sixth Avenue, I saw a figure at the entrance of the alley. It was Pierre. He followed me up the stairs and into my room, where the fire was almost out. "*Je te croyais morte*," he said and burst into sobs.

The next morning he clung to me as if he did not want me out of his sight for a moment. Already I had given him up. He had to be away on Monday and Tuesday and was dining out on Wednesday. Thursday was his last night, and he had saved it for me. I prepared a meal in front of the fire, but we were both without appetite.

"*Tu ne m'oublieras pas?*" he said, a look of pleading in his eyes, and when I did not answer, "*Dis-moi, ma petite, tu n'as pas d'autre amant?*"

I burst into peals of laughter.

"*Mais c'est horrible à rire.*"

"I had a lover, but now I have none."

He regarded me with so suffering an expression that I was moved. I wished that he had not looked at me in this way.

With lips, with tremulous flesh, with fervent, tender vows men and women dream to achieve a miracle, but every soul is impenetrable to every other soul. This is the inescapable tragedy of all human life.

We parted in the street. He went to gather his baggage, for he was sailing at noon, and I went on to my office.

It was the nights I dreaded most. I would lie awake for hours as if all my nerves had flame running through them, my hearing so acute that the sound of an elevated train would reach me from far in the distance. Yet, above the anguish of my thoughts, like an illuminated shrine in a sacked city, my intellect told me that it would pass, that everything passed, that nothing mattered; all was in the end as if it had never been, joy and sorrow were equally delusions.

I would sometimes dress and go out as the first glimmer of dawn showed at my window, and suddenly all my suffering would leave me and an exquisite serenity would take its place, as if I had escaped from some dark cavern into a world of transcendent light. But this did not last for long, and then the thought of death would drive in upon me, assailing me from every quarter. Each face into which I looked had mortality written across it. Even the flesh of a baby in the arms of its mother would shrivel and I would see the skeleton beneath. Everything in nature perished and was no more, the dogs following at their masters' heels, the cats at the ash bins, the very insects in the air, death claimed all. Nature contained not a form that was constant. We lived in the perilous center of an enigma, an enigma urgent and inscrutable. Death threw me back on life, life threw me back on death. I was pinned between the two. Then, suddenly, I would see a pigeon fluttering up from a roof top, with the light shining on its wings, or some other lovely manifestation of life, and all the rapture of the vanished hours – bitter-sweet, false-true – would flood up into my heart.

I received a cable from Pierre on his arrival in France, and soon after, some love poems. I do not know what turned the tide of my despair. There is, I suppose, in all human beings an irrepressible instinct towards life, something that raises us up against our knowledge, or even against our will.

I always retained a painful, complicated, and tender feeling for Pierre and a gratitude for the happiness he had given me, as well as for the suffering that had opened my eyes to the uncertain foundations on which our joys are reared. I did not blame him for his deception of me, knowing that we are all sports of nature. We had remained mysterious to each other to the end. Perhaps we parted at just the right moment. When I heard of his death some years before the beginning of this last war, my memory of our hours together returned full of a poetic sadness, purged of all bitterness. Bitterness is an acid that will destroy the sweetest fruits, and if our pride does not guard us against it our wisdom should.

Chapter XXVI

A BUSINESS VENTURE

AFTER Pierre's departure, I threw myself into my work with desperation. I would listen to stories from old Italians of their childhood in Tuscan villages or Sicilian vineyards as if they were tales from Cervantes or Verga. Brought over to America by their married sons and daughters, these old couples would arrive, apprehensive and bewildered in their peasant costumes, to be dropped into narrow rooms in sordid streets, with nothing to occupy them. Their grandchildren, taught at their schools that America was superior to all nations on the face of the globe, daily saluting the Stars and Stripes and shouting out their allegiance, would regard these progenitors of theirs with a derisive shame, as if they had come from some legendary, rather comic land. Yet there clung about these old people an atmosphere of a riper, more poetical culture that set them above their rude descendants. My entrance among them was greeted with a touching delight. The fact that I had been to their country, that I spoke their language, that I treated them with respect lent them new importance with the younger generation.

My work brought me into contact with the more influential, as well as with the humbler, of the Italian communities. It was like seeing a nation struggling to survive within a nation. I used sometimes to dine with the editor of one of the Italian newspapers and his wife in their dim rooms, far uptown. He was a man of vivacious intelligence, and she had charm and distinction. He gave me a letter of introduction to an Italian cardinal, a very old man, who received me in his scarlet robes – like an effigy carried down through the ages. I had been allowed to look upon an old masterpiece as it was about to crumble to dust.

The Waldensian minister, whom I visited on another occasion, was in the full vigor of his manhood. He showed me photographs of the Waldensian church at Piedmont, where his home had been, and gave me an eloquent account of the antiquity of this sect and of the persecutions to which it had been subjected.

I was visiting a Sicilian colony one day and was quickly surrounded by a friendly crowd. One of the women invited me to her rooms to have a glass of wine, and a procession followed after. During our conversation I referred to the *Mafia* and realized by the silence my words caused that I had blundered. When I returned to Milligan Place that afternoon, I was startled to discover a skull and crossbones with the word VENGEANCE painted in broad black strokes on my door. I made inquiries of the old men in Mr. Smith's shop, who, gratified at the sensation, told me they had seen two "rum customers" go in and out of the alley and had wondered what they could be up to. I had been suspected of spying out *Mafia* activities, for so great was the terror of this ring that the mere word could still excite people's fears.

Towards the end of the winter the study had been completed, and the results were brought out later in a series of publications.

I was once more without work and without plans. My friend Linda had thought up a scheme for starting a tea and flower shop, one which would be unique of its kind, and which would soon make us rich enough to retire for the rest of our days. She had already picked out a place, a little old two-story house on the corner of Seventh Avenue and Eleventh Street. A Spanish couple lived in it and were willing to rent the ground floor and basement to us at a reasonable sum. It was next to a large stable and had a quaint, stranded look on the wide, populous avenue with its modern business buildings.

I had saved a hundred dollars, and Linda, who knew the second-hand shops and auction rooms in every quarter of the city, set out to collect the furnishings, I following resistlessly in her wake.

Soon old men and old women and little boys were delivering on their handbarrows a remarkable assortment of copper trays, teapots of every size and shape, valuable cups without saucers, valuable saucers without cups, tables, round or square, high or low. With each one there was something missing or needing adjustment, but Linda assured me that it was as easy as lacing one's boots to get them into order, and they were all certainly astonishing bargains. What we lacked was made up from the five-and-ten cent store.

There was space in the tearoom for six tables. A narrow

stairway led down to a large basement where we had a gas cooking stove and a food safe. We had been told that rats sometimes got into the house, so we secured a sleek black cat with topaz eyes, but as we were trying to tempt him with a saucer of milk, he bolted up the stairs into our landlord's quarters, leaped like a flying lemur from an open window, and we never saw him again. Our shop took on a more and more individual look. It was, as Linda had predicted, different from all other shops.

Before continuing with the account of my sole venture into business, I must mention two friends who played an important part in my life at this time.

Henry Hoyt was a painter and a poet, a man of dashing appearance, with a brown mustache, thick eyebrows over large dark, beautiful eyes that evaded a direct glance, and a great deal of chestnut-colored hair brushed back from a low, troubled brow. He wore his clothes like a man of fashion and an adventurer, combining style with an indifference to style, and often with a touch of the fantastic – a necktie of bright-colored crepe paper, and a flower in his buttonhole to match. He came of an old American family, and his father had been a noted judge. He had volunteered as an air pilot in the war and had discovered on returning home that fate, in his absence, had dealt him a blow more cruel than any received in battle.

To me he was so spontaneously, so disarmingly friendly – unless that was his subtle way of being kind – that a day never passed without his searching me out. He helped us to get our shop into order, giving me some of his etchings to hang on the walls. He brought over his carpenter's tools and mended our furniture, fetching and carrying with an inexhaustible flow of paradoxical witticisms. He knew everyone in the smart literary and artistic circles, but he was like a tightrope walker who fears to glance to either side lest he lose his balance.

The other friend had been introduced to me by Randolph Bourne, though we later discovered that we had met as children at my Uncle Nat's, who had been a classmate of his father's at Harvard. Scofield Thayer was an only child and had always been wealthy. He lived on the top floor of an apartment house on Washington Square, where he had his bookshelves filled with rare first editions and Aubrey Beardsley drawings on his walls. Opposite an antique Chinese cabinet was a high, narrow window seat, covered with shabby leather, on which one perched as on one of these benches provided for lepers in medieval churches. The monk and the aesthete joined hands. He had an intellectual Japanese man-servant, a subscriber to the *Nation*, who, to salve his outraged pride, would sometimes enter the room backwards.

When Randolph had first mentioned Scofield Thayer to me, it was with warnings that I must curb any irrelevant witticisms. I came later to believe that he was one of those men the key to whose nature is so obscurely hidden that they alienate people because they remain outside their understanding. He was as sensitive to noise as was Proust and paid a monthly sum to the family living under him to turn off their gramophone at his will. In his summer home, at Cape Cod, he made a bargain with the owners of motor boats to muffle their engines. Alas! What fortune could today be vast enough to protect the most princely of the senses against the cunning torture of the machine? Scofield was himself a daring yachtsman and would, like Guy de

Maupassant, exult in steering his adventurous cutter through turbulent seas.

Slender of build, swift of movement, always strikingly pale, with coal-black hair, black eyes veiled and flashing, and lips that curved like those of Lord Byron, he seemed to many the embodiment of the aesthete with overrefined tastes and sensibilities. This was far from the case. Art and letters he pursued, but it was with a purpose so elevated and so impassioned that he remained insulated from the ironical comments about him. He suspected, however, the whole world, and it was perhaps this general distrust as betrayed by the carriage of his head and the timbre of his voice, that created about him an attitude of strain. He had, as Freud confirmed in speaking to me of him much later, a most gentle heart. He administered his wealth largely as a trust, supporting or helping to support many young writers and artists. He dressed with a considered simplicity, pleased to be seen in a suit of clothes he had worn since his university days. What were taken for affectations were mannerisms indigenous to his character. His irony, though as swift as Randolph's, was seldom as light. He was ice on the surface and molten lava underneath.

It was shortly after I knew Scofield Thayer that he became editor of *The Dial* magazine, which he bought with Dr. Watson from its former owners. After Pierre returned to France, he came frequently to see me, and a friendship developed between us. The hours I spent with him were never dull, though they might on occasion be nervous. Like most people of distinction he was often egocentric, though not egotistical; his courtesy could be exquisite and he was touchingly susceptible to the words of the people he valued. His mind was inflammable and satirical, and it was at the same time sober and sad. He defended himself with his wit, the best way of banishing fear. Like Diderot, he would rather be impatient than bored, and he alternated between the tempest and the frozen lake. He never felt wholly at ease in America. With few exceptions, he preferred his English friends.

Chapter XXVII

LIBERATION

THE morning our shop was to open, I received word from Mrs. Dale, Linda's mother, that Linda had been taken ill. I hurried to lay in the day's provisions, then boarded an uptown car to make my purchase of flowers. The proprietors of the wholesale flower establishments were laconic, avaricious men, as impervious to the appeal of the fragile blossoms they flung down like dice on a counter as tigers to a minuet. One, more honest than the others, whispered in my ears when I asked him the price of some lilies, "You can have them cheap, but they will be dead in an hour." These words, with the implication so clear, had a strangely horrifying effect upon me which lingered for long afterwards. It always remained distressing to me to see these men, their cigars sticking out of their mouths, and their hats on the backs of their heads, standing amidst the lovely scented flowers, fresh in from silent hothouses, and now subjected to the gross pawings of these urban wolves of commerce.

I can describe this period of my life only as a perpetual nightmare, redeemed by the presence of Henry Hoyt, who spent most of his day helping me, and of his friend, William Rose Benét, the poet, with whom he lived, and his brother Stephen Benét. These young men would arrive in the late afternoon, clattering down my stairs like schoolboys, singing snatches of song, and reciting snatches of poetry. They would wash up my dishes as if they were playing an exciting game, or as if one had the cymbals, the other the tambour, and the third the drum – allegretto spiritoso, prestissimo, scherzando. All would be finished in a moment, the weight that had been bearing down upon me would suddenly lift and my tiredness be forgotten. We would have dinner at a nearby Hungarian restaurant; then we would part and I would go to Linda's. Her illness had developed into double pneumonia, and her mother had no one to help her.

The offices of *The Dial* magazine were two blocks from my shop, and Scofield and Dr. Watson would frequently come in for tea, bringing manuscripts to discuss. There was a small window in my basement that was like a peephole in a dungeon through which I squinted up into the free world above. When I saw these two delightful and distinguished young men about to enter my shop, I would wish that I might be invisibly transported to the Bougainville Island, so commended by Diderot. This absurdly shameful feeling gave me insight into the psychology of people doing menial work while others, more fortunate, conversed over their yellow chartreuse about the habits of the Golden Fye, or whether Sören Kierkegaard or Po Chu-i had grasped the true secret of the universe. Of course a philosopher who is a true philosopher should be always a philosopher, but "it is not given to the children of men to be philosophers without envy."

I would sometimes catch sidelong glances from the large, expressive eyes of Dr. Watson – the most expressive eyes I have ever encountered. He was tall and strikingly good-looking, with fair hair, a fair mustache, and unusually beautiful hands. But perhaps the most unusual thing about him was the quality of his silence, a silence so charged with perception, so poised on intensity, so subtly and evasively provocative that it was difficult to tell whether it was offered as a lure to oneself or constiuted his own sole means of escape.

The habitués of my shop ranged from derelict characters, to whom, in a benevolent, idle moment I sometimes offered a free cup of tea, to women of fashion who entered my door as if they were putting their foot in a fox's gin. Among the former was a tall, lean Irishman called Patrick. He had a nose nearly as long as his narrow countenance, that seemed to be prying its way into everything about him while he plotted tirelessly how to secure enough money to buy himself a bottle of "hooch" – a cheap liquor, unlawfully sold. I would give him jobs to do and thus make him work out what he had wheedled from me. Some of the old men from whom we had bought our furniture would come in to find out how business was going, eyeing regretfully their tables and chairs, now polished and mended. Artists, writers, lovers, truck drivers, settlement workers, laborers, sharpers – all kinds came and went.

My mother spent a night with me. She looked sadly but bravely about my shop and said she never had known what I would do next. As for the profits promised by Linda, it needed, apparently, her enterprise to secure them. I would find at the end of each night from twenty to thirty dollars in the cash-box, all of which would have vanished the following morning after I had replenished my stores. I had always cunningly evaded housework, and now I found myself plunged in so deep that I could think of nothing but the weariness of my limbs.

I do not know how much longer I should have continued to hold out if something had not occurred to force me to a speedy decision. I had heard for a long time strange sounds in the wainscoting of the walls, as if pygmy giants were carrying on riotous sports. The man next door to me said that his stable was full of rats, "bouncing fellows, as big as buffaloes," that frightened his cat, Floss. He had already caught several "great ruffians" in a trap. I kept all the food locked up at night and was careful to leave no crumbs about.

One afternoon I had just brought up a tray with tea for some customers and was returning down the stairs, when to my consternation I saw the kitchen literally swarming with rats. Some were running off with rolls, others snatching at food. I clapped my hands until all had scampered away, like mutineers on a ship awaiting a better opportunity for their mischief. When Henry Hoyt and our other friends arrived, I told them of my adventure and on the spot took down my sign and decided to earn my living in some more safe and agreeable manner.

Bill Benét was so concerned for me that he said he would give me work on the *Saturday Review of Literature*, of which he was then assistant editor. Remembering my difficulty in writing about my visit to the tugboat, I was fearful of accepting his offer, but I never forgot this so characteristic action of his; and I may say here that I have never, in all my experience, met a man more magnanimous, more good, in the true and simple use of this much abused word, than this gifted, modest, and charming poet.

All my friends were going away. Scofield and Paul Rosenfeld had already left for their summer homes, and Henry Hoyt would soon go to his mother in Maine. His extravagantly high spirits had suddenly deserted him, and his expression had so altered that it was painful to be with him. He would sit in my rooms without uttering a word, some blight at the core of his being. I used to bring in Neapolitan ices, and he would eat them passively, obediently, without pleasure. My nature being one of extremes – "melancholy without cause and merry against the hair" – I could understand something of this abrupt change. It was a melancholy that accompanied his every act and colored the whole universe about him, and "melancholy is the nurse of frenzy." It was with heavy hearts that his friends saw him off on his so-called holiday.

Chapter XXVIII

IN THE CAGE

I HAD to make haste to find some means of earning my living. I went to call on Stephanie, who had moved to a house she was sharing with a friend. This friend was employed by the Chatfield-Taylor Company, an advertising firm, and said that some extra people were required in the statistical department for temporary work. The word statistical made me hesitate, but Stephanie assured me that it was merely a matter of a little subtraction and addition which anyone could do. I decided to apply and was given a place with other workers at a table as long as the gambling tables at Monte Carlo. The sums were not difficult, and I managed to come through the ordeal without disgrace.

The heat was so intense during these weeks that on reaching my rooms I would mount a little iron ladder, push up a trap door, and come out onto a flat roof where I could breathe in all the air there was. I used frequently to sleep on this roof. The Italian grocer, Mr. Feraggio, who lived next door to me, was the only other inhabitant of the alley to avail himself of this privilege. He would bring up his pillow and I would bring up mine. In the daytime he would assume his respectful shopman's manner, but up under the free stars he could stretch himself like any sheik. I never experienced in Naples, or even in the West Indies, anything to compare with New York heat. There were occasions when the offices remained closed and the entire population lay as immobile as the crocodiles at the aquarium. Only Joe, the iceman, would hop about at his trade with a spry and cheerful cupidity.

To my alarm and surprise, I was offered permanent work in the statistical department of the Chatfield-Taylor Company. It seemed that the wife of the president had taken a fancy to me. She was a beautiful woman, with the spontaneous charm of a Lady Hamilton. She had a veneration for the arts and was a strong feminist. Mr. Chatfield, her husband, combined with a razor-edge business capacity an adoration for his wife, and he satisfied all her whims up to the point where they might interfere with his larger profits.

The Chatfield-Taylor Company occupied five stories of an enormous sixteen-story office building. The statistical department was on the fifth floor. At the head of it was a young woman who had not only a statistical mind but an imaginative one. She was from Nebraska, and her name was Nancy. I made up my mind on our first meeting that she would see me through. I was given a large, important-looking desk, surrounded by adding machines, which I eyed with a combination of distrust and hope.

My task was to compile a book of trade statistics. The work was less complicated than exacting and tedious. It was as remote from my natural tastes and abilities as anything could possibly be, but Nancy and I soon developed a friendship that compensated for everything. It was based largely on humor and a love of gossip, gossip that had as its foundation a criticism of life.

We were surrounded by odd characters, from Dominic, the

modest Italian elevator man in his gray livery, to the president himself, passing with rapid, self-engrossed strides to his private office, the very embodiment of power and authority. The whole atmosphere of the Chatfield-Taylor Company was that of an evangelical institution formed for the sole purpose of spreading prosperity and enlightenment among the masses, while, underneath, like a swordfish in deep waters, sagacious and predatory, stirred the competitive push of big business.

This is not to say that there was any overt hypocrisy on the parts of the directors of the company. They were sincere, humane men – as these words are commonly used – but they had sold themselves to themselves so effectively that not a rift remained to let through the light. Having secured the best brains, the best manners, the most clever, versatile, and accommodating people in the market to work for them, they were assiduous to keep up the tone, and everyone else, with fat salaries in his pockets, was equally assiduous. Failures in the literary world, indigent young writers down-at-the-heel and hoping to repair their fortunes by a few obsequious pen strokes, were quickly disposed of. But those writers that professed to have given up a successful literary career because of the irresistible appeal of business were offered a chance. When poets can keep off starvation by whittling down their caprices, why should they not polish their shoes and send in their applications? No one likes to die of starvation, not even poets.

Later I was able to obtain interviews for two most rare poets – Elinor Wylie and Hart Crane.

The firm employed a psychologist of international repute, a man with so remarkable a mind that it used to distress me to consider the purposes to which he was putting it. He had, however, been forced to resign his professorship from the university where he was teaching because of a love affair, and if the great bodies of academic learning think best to thrust out their most original thinkers because of a few artless indiscretions, the business world is not so finical. Later I used to go into this man's office to consult with him and would remain to argue. He had a mind as lucid as rain water in a crock, and had everything thought out from *A* to Z, the only omission being a solution of the enigma of life and death, which science leaves to the idle religious.

Nancy and I, being privileged workers, had no one to supervise us, and we would sometimes steal out and get an ice cream soda. One lovely sunny morning we rode on the top of a bus to Grant's Tomb. Nancy was a girl of the strictest probity and would have spoken out at any time rather than betray her principles, but we were both, in our small way, philosophers. Whom could it harm, as long as our work got done, if we spent a fraction of our employer's time in innocent enjoyment? I was astonished, as far as that goes, that my task, with Nancy's help, progressed as it did. I could now handle an adding machine as easily as an umbrella and wished that I might never be without one.

The sheets were at last sent off to the printer, the proofs returned and checked up by Nancy and me; and a slim volume, bound in calf's skin leather, with gilt edges, a silk marker, and my name embossed on it in gold letters, was finally placed before me. Instead of feeling pride and pleasure, I felt a vague uneasiness. I had got my total state populations from the official census reports, while my trade statistics had, in many cases, come from lists sent to me by union officials. In casting my eyes anxiously and responsibly over these various totals, I was suddenly frozen to my chair to discover that in one of the states the number of people employed in a certain single trade exceeded the entire population of the state. I rushed to Nancy to point out this horrifying discrepancy. She burst into laughter and comforted me by saying that mistakes were bound to creep in, and that she was sure not one person in a hundred would notice it.

Still championed by Mrs. Chatfield, who was ever my fairy godmother, I was suddenly promoted to the copy department. One of the girls working with me was a brilliant scholar. Her father was a noted philosopher who had been an associate of William James.

It used to amaze me to see the sober, dedicated countenances of the men and women about me, the long rows of checkers and draftsmen (there was a list of a thousand artists waiting to have their work considered), the well-appointed library. The firm was a strictly honorable one. It would advertise no goods the reliability of which it had not thoroughly investigated, but the ethics of advertising as such were as rigorously defended as is the Christian religion by Pope or Baptist minister.

And what was the end of all this elaborate and frenzied activity? One had but to glance through the pages of any popular magazine. It was a mock world that advertising presented, a papier-mâché world of show and pretense, veiling snobbishness, lust, rapacity, and vacuity of mind.

My nature revolted against the copy I was called upon to write. Of course advertisers were not supposed to be revolutionary reformers or great sages, and having at their service the sharpest brains in the business world, they could prove that advertising was of the greatest benefit to humanity. Anything can be proved by logic, anything but that logic bears any relation to truth.

I never did fit satisfactorily into the requirements of the Chatfield-Taylor Company, but I was surrounded by so many generous and helpful people, ready to cover up my lapses and give me fresh encouragement, that I managed to cling on somehow. I had got in by an error and remained in by a miracle. That is not to say that I did not keep my eyes open to what was going on about me. Mr. Taylor, the other partner of the firm, used to give us lectures on the "secrets" of advertising. He was a dapper man, with a mind as unruffled by speculation as a sewing machine. The narrow strip of plush carpet leading from the elevator to his large private office, where his secretary, trig and chatty, awaited him each morning, represented the width of his intellectual horizon. It used to seem incongruous to me that I should be made to take orders from such a man. Yet, so insidious is the effect of power and success over even civilized minds that his nonchalant assumption of superiority could create in me a sensation of impotence and humiliation, a feeling that helped me to understand the psychology of workers compressing all their talents into one channel for the glory and affluence of their employers.

Chapter XXIX

THE DOOR OPENS

In the late autumn, Henry Hoyt returned from his visit to his mother, appearing suddenly in my rooms. Sparks of his old gaiety would come up and be quickly extinguished, and his efforts at response were strained.

I lay on my couch, reading, one evening, when I heard footsteps running up the stairs. It was Bill Benét, who, with anxious face, asked me whether I had seen Henry. He had found the door of their apartment locked and had been unable to fit the key into the keyhole. He rushed away and I followed after him. The door was forced open, and we found Henry lying dead upon the floor. In the preternatural stillness of the room his army wrist watch could be distinctly heard ticking, and I do not know why the regular beat of this ingenious mechanism brought home to me in so invincible a manner a sense of mortality. In a story of Dostoevsky's, a husband, alone in the room with his dead wife, communicates a similar emotion: "The pendulum of the clock keeps beating, but it is not needed now, no one needs it, no one is here but sorrow."

In a moment the room was swarming with people. They seemed to spring up out of space, from nowhere, as if they had been hiding behind curtains or under the furniture, waiting for a signal to appear – coroner, policemen, and a whole army of young reporters with note books and pencils held in readiness, each vying with the other in getting a good "story." They were all, undoubtedly, kind young men at heart, but like barbers and grocery clerks they had to earn a living, and a suicide, especially that of a gifted, handsome young artist, member of a rich and noted family, made first-rate copy. "What beast couldst thou be that were not subject to a beast?"

Bill Benét was so struck to the heart, so bewildered and shattered, that he could not articulate a single word and scarcely realized what was going on about him, and these young men directed all their attention upon me. When they inquired about Henry's family, I told them that one of his sisters was the wife of the Baron . . . . ., mentioning a name of international interest at that time, now gone from my mind.

This has always seemed to me one of the most shameful occurrences of my life. When I reached home, the distress I felt over it drove even my grief momentarily from my thoughts – the fact that I was able, with my friend lying stark in tragic death only a few yards from me, to allow to pass my lips, as a concession to a crew of prying strangers, some boast about an eminent family connection. When I have been with people who have volunteered to tell the worst actions of their lives, this incident has returned to accuse me. I could never bring myself to recount it and do so now for the first time.

The burial service took place at one of those withering crematory chapels where the sermon seems to be run off like numbers on the stock exchange. How preferable is the custom of the Hindus, who burn their dead on pyres in the open air! Only the pale face of Bill Benét gave me back insight into the true values of life – fidelity to a friend, depth of generous emotion, and humility before the inexorable strokes of fate.

On the return of Scofield from his summer holiday, we resumed our friendship. Sometimes we would dine in a small restaurant nearby, sometimes in a smart uptown restaurant, where the waiters, concealing the anxiety and poverty of their days behind a deferential mask, would rush forward to serve us.

The unreliability of the senses may be somewhat measured by the way the outer scene is forever taking on different meanings according to our age and circumstance. When, as a child, I used to dine at a fashionable restaurant with my Uncle Nat, I would be intimidated by the elegance of the women as they moved so confidently to their places. They would seem to inhabit a more privileged world than my own. When in later years I was invited out to dine with Paul Rosenfeld, I would feel as if I were in the center of a Balzac novel, surrounded by fascinating couples carrying on subtle intrigues. With Pierre, though everything drove sharply in on my perceptions, yet all remained as remote as if viewed through glass, as distinct and at the same time as unreal as if I were in a dream. Now, with Scofield, I would once more look about me and this time I would see on each countenance traces of futility and pretence. Then my eye would return to the pale, classical features of my friend.

In the mid-summer of this year he made up his mind to go abroad. The evening before he was to sail, we had dinner at an outdoor restaurant, and as the weather was unusually breathless, seated ourselves on a bench in Washington Square. What remained most strongly with me afterwards was a sense of sadness. For of what use is it to be young, gifted, distinguished, privileged to move freely over the globe if joy is out of reach?

> Their breath is agitation and their life
> A storm whereon they ride.

It was not long before his letters began to come, usually dictated, with comments crowded about the margins in his unbalanced, imperious handwriting. He had got it into his head that if I would be his secretary the difficulties of his days would entirely disappear. But no amount of money, no promise of a life of ease – traveling through the most beautiful countries of Europe, meeting the most illustrious people – could tempt me from my dusty alley. I was convinced that I would fall far short of his expectations, and I valued my freedom above all other things. Cablegrams would arrive, but I would hold firm, seizing one excuse and then another. I said I was busy collecting material for a book on Jane Welsh Carlyle, and it was true that I had such a book in mind and would frequently spend my evenings in the reference rooms of the Public Library reading about this celebrated and tedious couple.

I had by this time saved some money and determined to give up my position and make an effort to support myself by writing. I had small hope of succeeding, but it seemed insufferable to go on prodding my wits to such ends. My attention was always wandering towards a large clock that hung just within range of my eye. The hands of this clock seemed to remain stationary or to move so imperceptibly that my life would sink and disappear as I contemplated it, and a deadly torpor overtake me. If the end of life was to experience, and one experienced only drowsiness, escape seemed imperative.

What astonished me was the docility of human beings. The lower-paid workers moved as unresistingly to their places as toy soldiers. We more privileged employees could rise and stretch ourselves and exchange jests. We had a whole margin of freedom not enjoyed by the others, yet I often thought that if I had had some simple task like sorting buttons, or polishing silver – though that is rather strenuous – something that left my mind free for rumination while earning me just enough to pay for my food and rent, I would have been happier.

To be sure, wherever human beings are, there also is the possibility of drama. I would be asked on occasion to return to the office after dinner to consult with the famous producer of a film, soon to be shown, that played up the virtues of motherhood. I was the copy writer for this film, but I collaborated with one of the "representatives." In advertising, the representative holds a position equal in importance to that of an elder of the Moravian Church. This young man could bring out as many pat ideas as there are quills on a porcupine's back. He was spruce, persuasive – *copia verborum* – and looked very much like an advertisement himself.

The producer was a Jew and was more sympathetic to me, though he was as sharp as a hairpin and resembled one of those peddlers that appear at one's back door with some rare antique to sell, wrapped negligently in a piece of old newspaper. He had a silk polka dot handkerchief which he kept pulling from his sleeve as a magician pulls out a white rabbit. His attitude towards the public was as simple as that of a baker towards his dough, or a barber towards his strop. He was cynical and ingratiating, and there was about him a touch of the exotic that lent variety to life.

The representative, keeping up the best tradition of the company, wished to stress the "uplift" effect of the film, as if it had been written by a group of philanthropists for the sole purpose of benefiting humanity. Had not every man a mother? And every woman, too, for that matter, and every mouse, and every jenny wren, and every scurrying cockroach, though they did not come into it. Mr. G . . . . . calculated all in terms of dollars and cents and saw through life as if it had been a child's hoop.

I used to be so engrossed studying these two that I failed entirely to attend to their words and would acquiesce first with one and then with the other, feeling very much like an impostor myself. But presently I would get weary and would want to go home. We were not paid for our extra hours of work, it being taken as a matter of course that loyalty to the firm stood above our own personal caprices. Sometimes, after these conferences, I would not turn out my light until two o'clock in the morning and would have to be back at my desk at the usual hour.

All these side views on my days I shared, in snatched moments, with Nancy, and my chief regret in leaving the company was that I should have to say good-bye to her and to other friends I had made. Indeed, I feel now a certain shame when I think of all the gifted and attractive people who seemed to experience so little of my own rebellion in the great gilded cage that enclosed them, and from whom I had received nothing but kindness.

As I was taken down in the elevator for the last time by Dominic, with the brass buttons of his livery shining like those of a field marshal, it was with no sense of triumph that I looked back upon the two years I had spent with the Chatfield-Taylor Company. It seemed the merest chance that I was leaving of my own accord. My time had not been wholly without profit, however. I had learned to write a sentence as bare as a peeled withe and as hard-hitting as a boy's fist, and I had seen a side of life I should otherwise never have known. I had ascertained that the human mind, like the chameleon, can change color according to circumstance, and that success in the world of affairs bears little relation to the inner harmony of the spirit.

> . . . therefore it is meet
> That noble minds keep ever with their likes;
> For who so firm that cannot be seduced?

Chapter XXX

A PRECARIOUS LIVELIHOOD

Almost simultaneously with my newly acquired liberty I received a notice asking me to give up my rooms. This was a possibility that had never occurred to me. It was like being projected out of a safe harbor into the open sea. Cornelia told me she was sure the landlord would rent me a floor in Patchin Place, and her words proved true, but the rent was higher, and the rooms dark and on a ground floor.

Linda knew an Irishman, Mr. Bradley, who, she said, would do all my moving for me. He was "as strong as granite" and very good-natured as well. He did, indeed, look as if he might have hoisted the whole alley onto his shoulders. He was a giant of a man, with crisply curling fair hair and a guileless smile, and when, after Linda's introduction, we shook hands, my mangled fingers gave me sure proof, had I needed any, of his prowess. He had not, however, come for an afternoon's chat, and looking about him, he started at once to work, seizing hold of my mahogany table and piling upon it rugs, cushions, and blankets, with a brass coal scuttle perched dizzily at the summit of all. To reach my new quarters he had several devious turns to make and a wide courtyard to cross.

I became more and more concerned for my blankets, which were trailing in the dust, and when I saw my coal scuttle about to fall, I ventured a word of warning to Mr. Bradley, who had his head turned upwards as if searching the heavens for the signs of the zodiac. He came to an abrupt halt, while my coal scuttle clattered onto the courtyard – frightening two cats about to fly at each other's throats.

"Excuse me, Miss," he said, "if you don't mind me mentioning it. You make me nervous. If you'll just leave it all to me, I'll get 'em over, but I'm of a nervous temperament and I'm apt to break things if I'm spoken to."

I decided to take his advice and did not go into my new rooms until the last object had been deposited there. The floors and walls had been freshly painted, and with Linda's and Mrs. Carroll's aid everything was at last got into order. There was a warm coal fire, and my spirits began to rise.

When I woke the following morning, it was snowing. From where I lay in my bed, I could see the flakes, small and dry, falling ceaselessly down behind the little square window panes, and this sight gave me an unaccountable joy. I would have liked to remain all the rest of my days in that delicious state of suspended consciousness where age could never overtake me, death was illusory, the loss of love innocuous, and poverty impossible. I felt as if I had some power that could make harmless every sting of fate. When Cardinal Newman said that man was not a reasoning animal, but a seeing, contemplating, acting one, I am sure he spoke truly. Reason is no more than our weapon of defense.

What days of luxury these first free days from my office were! Each moment was a gift that I could touch and treasure and put away for recollection. I was determined to make every effort to avoid being caught in such a trap ever again.

I called on Bill Benét at the *Saturday Review of Literature*, where he received me with his usual geniality, handing me out at once a book to review. It was by a French writer, Henri Bordeaux, whose name was then unknown to me. I hurried up to the Public Library and went through the entire collected works of this celebrated *campagnard*. When, after my marriage, I happened to be staying in the village in the Savoy, where he had lived and died. I searched out a venerable servant of his, who was touchingly pleased to tell me stories of her "good master." The review took me a long time to write, and I received fifteen dollars for it. Of no money have I ever been so proud.

The next thing I attempted was an essay on Leopardi. This I sent to *Vanity Fair* and was truly startled at the efficiency of a post office service that could get it back again into my hands with so weird a dexterity. It was accompanied with a polite letter from the literary editor, Mr. Edmund Wilson. In the end this essay came out in a university publication, with its immaturities embalmed in good printers' ink. I then did a satire on advertising which was published in the *New Republic*, and Van Wyck Brooks, whom I had known as a friend of Randolph's, and who was now literary editor of the *Freeman*, frequently gave me books to review. So started my literary career – if it merits to be called such. It was a gambler's life, but perhaps a little better than robbing on the highway.

Words, words, words – how they mount up and mount up until, empty as they are, whole populations sink beneath their weight! They rush at us through the air and fill our nostrils like smoke; they perplex our wits and break our hearts: "to know what is hidden by onesided words, to know the pitfalls of wanton words, know the error of false words, and know the poverty of shuffling words." Benjamin Constant used to assert that he preferred painting to all literary composition because it dispensed with words which, he considered, spoiled whatever they sought to express. When Charlemagne was asked by his son what speech was, he is said to have answered, "The betrayer of the human soul"; and in Flaubert's peculiar words, "Human speech is like a cracked tin kettle on which we hammer out tunes to make bears dance when we want to move the stars." Yet it is only by these little messengers of deception that we may get outside ourselves and know what others think of a universe as strange as the one in which we live. "Thanks to art," writes Proust, "instead of seeing only one world, our own, we see it under multiple forms, and as many as there are original artists, just so many worlds have we at our disposal, differing more widely than those that roll in infinite space."

To make one's living by writing has usually, however, little enough to do with art. As soon as we mingle with the crowd, our most original insights are jostled from us. I was far from aspiring to be an artist. If I could find a place anywhere in the long procession of honest, anxious scribblers who earned a bare living in the literary market, I thought, I should be delighted. But I had neither a facile pen nor a disciplined mind. Any kind of literary composition I undertook seemed to end either in the suspended contemplation I have before alluded to, or a fruitless, painful effort at concentration from which, as Dr. Johnson puts it, "the attention is every moment starting to more delightful amusements."

I decided to make a study of some of the current magazines and went out to the nearest newsstand, returning with a selection under my arm. But if I found concentration difficult when engaged in literary composition, it now appeared to elude me even more. When I did get swept resistlessly along, like dust in a swirling gutter, I felt such disaffection for all authorship, such withering distaste for life, that I almost decided to give up my intention forever and go in for some more ingenuous task.

It was at this time that I got from the library some of the prose writings of Matthew Arnold, and they gave me back my serenity. I know that Matthew Arnold has been much derided as a critic – notably by Swinburne; but if one does not always come out at the place one might desire with him, one is conscious of being in the company of a man both honest and imaginative. The popular magazine, like the radio, reflects the intellectual and literary modes of the hour instead of seeking to uncover any realities of life. It is the fashion plate of the spinning mind.

During all this time, Scofield had not abandoned his hope of persuading me to be his secretary. Since nothing seemed to avail against my mysterious obstinacy, a new idea supplanted this one in his mind. *The Dial*, with its high aesthetic aims and its disregard of any wide popular appeal, was a heavy financial burden for him and Dr. Watson to carry. Mr. Gilbert Seldes, who was then managing editor, was about to give up his position, and Scofield – always with the same alarming and ungrounded idea of my ability – thought that with my literary tastes, at once adventurous and old-fashioned, and my special knowledge of advertising I would make a lucky successor. He consulted Dr. Watson who gave his consent.

But if the idea of being a secretary was disconcerting to me, the idea of being an editor was even more so. The difficulty of refusing appeared almost equal, however, to that of accepting. It was a dazzling offer, for editors are looked up to as monarchs in the world of letters; though "some editors are scrubs, mere drudges, newspaper puffs; others are bullies and quacks; others nothing at all – they have the name and receive a salary for it." Yet to pass from a poor discouraged writer straight into the editorial chair was like being invited up from the hold of a great ocean liner to occupy the suite of honor on the promenade deck. I held out, none the less, still prizing humble liberty above "tottering honor."

Late one evening I heard footsteps, followed by a knock at my door. To my surprise I saw Scofield, accompanied by Dr. Watson. I had known that he would be back from Europe at about this time but did not suppose he would come to see me without first telephoning. They seated themselves side by side on my divan, one so dark and erect, the other so fair and withdrawn. Scofield touched off the idiosyncrasies of some of the celebrities he had recently seen, from George Moore to Arthur Schnitzler, from Gertrude Stein to Virginia Woolf, in a manner as lively as the releasing of a trigger. He had evidently not been intimidated or seduced by anything the capitals of Europe could offer in their grab bag of sophistication to a young American aesthete, but had stored up his ironies to let them off in my little room like those "sparklers," the fire of which, Mr. T. F.

Powys tells us, will be the kind used in hell. The real purpose of this visit was to persuade me to change my mind about taking over the management of *The Dial*. I did not say I would not consent to so flattering an offer, which was equivalent to saying I would.

Chapter XXXI

THE DIAL MAGAZINE

NO SOONER was it known that I was to become the managing editor of *The Dial* than the world surrounding me appeared to undergo a singular transformation. Young men whose names I could hardly recall would take off their hats in the street with a wide sweep and a low bow. Invitations to parties were continually arriving.

Miss Amy Lowell, famous as a patroness of art and letters, wrote from her Concord home asking me to dine with her on her approaching visit to New York. This was arranged, and I went with a mutual friend to her hotel where, as it seemed, I had received a royal summons.

Miss Lowell had left word that we were to be shown to our table as she might be late. At her entrance, the waiters fell back as if for the passage of Mme. Tom Thumb or some other equally famous personage, and she took the chair held ready for her as it is said Queen Victoria took hers, without once glancing round. She was short of stature, round as a hamper, with a little head set firmly on her shoulders and gray hair gathered to a competent knot – as any busy housewife might dispose of straggling locks. Her dress was an exquisite creation of old-fashioned elegance – a stiff pearl-gray satin brocade with a fichu of lace that must have been a prized family heirloom.

Perhaps the word that could best describe Miss Lowell was the one she might herself have used: "perky." She did in some way suggest New England – its sagacity, energy, and pluck. She talked of the book she was writing on Keats, saying that she was from New England, where, when you undertook a thing, you did it thoroughly.

This book, because of its reception by the critics, is said to have been the final cause of Miss Lowell's death. She had intended it to be the crowning achievement of her life.

My form of nervousness is such that it is difficult for me to eat in company. I am apt to swallow furtively, as a dog snatches a bone and makes off with it when his master's back is turned. It is not that I do not enjoy good food, but the processes of eating and the rigors of social intercourse seem to me to accord ill together. This personal idiosyncrasy leaves my attention all the more free to take in what is confronting me, and I seemed to take in on this occasion all the aspects of Miss Lowell's character.

Swathed round and round in a truss of bandages under her crisp bodice – as Alexander Pope is said to have been swathed – she sat up, vital as a bandit, producing at the end of her meal one of the long black cigars that had so startled the dovecots of Boston Society. Was not George Sand equally a smoker of cheroots? But George Sand had had her lovers, and Miss Lowell, we must suppose, had missed this disturbing initiation. It was one of the few things requiring boldness and address that she had missed, for there was hardly a corner to which her inexhaustible, inquisitive enterprise and her New England conscience had not goaded her in pursuit of the quarry which, despite all her precautions, had in the end slipped so evasively through her net. But as I pictured her in her hotel bedroom that night, preparing herself for those long, dark hours of silent self-communing, I could envisage only a courageous and pathetic old woman, stripped of her armor, and anxiously meditating upon the next move in the strenuous battle ahead of her.

A poet very different from Miss Lowell was Miss Marianne Moore, whom Scofield had brought to have tea in my rooms. Slim and straight, dressed in a sober and original manner, with a mass of beautiful, fine, reddish hair, coiled in broad shining plaits about her small head, Miss Moore combined delicacy of observation with vigor of mind.

It has been said that wealth of intellect is what makes a man happy, and we may suppose the same to apply to a woman. Wealth of intellect is just what most characterizes Miss Moore – intellect disinterested and voracious, lingering in peculiar side-paths, storing all in the memory, disconnected yet relevant, excited yet attentive, and always animated with modesty and humor.

Later I was privileged to be accepted by her and her mother as a friend and used to visit them at St. Luke's Place, where an old-world atmosphere gave repose to their harmonious and hospitable rooms. I would not be giving a true picture of this eloquent poet did I not mention her courage, a courage that yields no inch to circumstance. I do not know whether she still wears the large hats with their broad brims that so became her and that I always associate with her. Even in the matter of dress she remained true to herself, and in ignoring the caprices of fashion, made those more slavish seem merely commonplace.

Publicity of any kind she retreated from and would rather hide her gifts, or cultivate them for her own enrichment, than compete in the open market where quality so quickly tarnishes and excellence so little matters.

The offices of *The Dial* magazine and *The Dial* Publishing Company occupied the whole of a large, old-fashioned, three-story house in a downtown residential section of the city, once fashionable, but now left to retiring old ladies, peering from behind dusty lace curtains onto the street below no longer populous as in their youth. The word *office* is hardly, however, a suitable one to describe the spacious, square, homely rooms, with their casual collection of shabby furniture – selected, apparently, as little for display as for efficiency. They had something of old New York still lingering about them, its serenity and its leisured dignity.

If I could see that I should be at ease in such a place, I could see equally that I should be happy with my assistant editor. I had once remarked Sophia Wittenberg walking on a summer evening hand in hand with a young man. I had not known who these fortunate lovers were but singled them out as the very flower of romance. Now I was to discover the young woman was none other than my new working companion, and that the young man was her husband, Lewis Mumford. Not only did Sophia have the rare and startling virtue of beauty, but she had the sweetness of nature that gives delight to that beauty and, to add a touch of the incredible, she was efficient as well.

The Dial Magazine

The Dial magazine held a peculiar place in American letters. Perhaps it could best be compared with the *Yellow Book* of the Nineties. Its interests were mainly literary and artistic, though the most noted philosophers of our generation were frequent contributors to its pages. Its claims were proud, which was enough to excite hostility. For two young men to devote their hearts, their fortunes, and their time to some entirely disinterested aim seemed sufficient to cause people, like rooks tumbled from their rookery, to chatter and peck.

Centuries of civilization have given European countries a riper culture than that of America, and a greater number of people who care for art as an indispensable portion of the common life. *The Dial*, in publishing the work of distinguished Europeans, such as Jules Romains, Thomas Mann, Roger Fry, George Santayana, D. H. Lawrence, Virginia Woolf, Paul Valèry, and Marcel Proust, sought to widen and instruct the taste of American readers, while encouraging native writers and poets with original talent to contribute to its pages. On the one hand it was critized for being too orthodox, and on the other, for being too experimental. Its drawings – particularly its Picassos – were thought fantastic, its poetry – Mr. Eliot's *The Waste Land* appeared first in its pages – obscure. Yet it was eagerly read by people living out of reach of cosmopolitan centers, who regarded it, with the intrepid *Little Review*, as their sole means of keeping in touch with the international world of art and letters. It published the early work of writers, poets, and artists whose names have since become famous.

When I assumed my position as managing editor of *The Dial*, I was intensely anxious to live up to my obligations. I had myself received in my mail some of those printed slips that shrivel the confidence of young writers, turning the golden light of the sun to "pitchy darkness," and I was loath to join the ranks of those demagogues of editors who disposed of nine-tenths of the manuscripts set out before them as if they were so many peanut husks, though, as the literary editor of a noted English weekly reminded me only recently, "A literary journal is no eleemosynary institution." An editor cannot spend all his peculiar and transitory hours composing letters to young literary aspirants who would end by filling his office with enough waste paper to set a whole town ablaze. What *The Dial* did draw the line at was allowing young poets to pull their poems from their hungry pockets to declaim at their leisure. Even Diderot, the most compassionate of philosophers, had finally to defend himself against such disquieting tactics, and Leopardi made the suggestion that if poets were determined on an audience, they should be made to pay for it. *The Dial* honored poets so much, however, that it paid them at twice the rate of its prose writers, thus reversing the general custom.

The top floor of the magazine was given up to a diningroom where the contributors could meet for a meal when they pleased, and where eminent authors and artists visiting New York were entertained for dinner, with Scofield's Japanese servant to take the place of cook and waiter.

Dr. Watson was apt to be absent on these occasions, and Scofield would preside at the head of the table, communicating by his air of frozen civility a feeling of constraint. When I remonstrated with him once, saying that I feared he had been bored, "Not bored, in torture," was his reply. Yet he could be the most delightful, and certainly the most brilliant, of companions. He had so high a standard and so imperious a manner that at the first sound of his voice everyone would stand at attention – as if Tiberius himself had set foot on the stair – though all were fond of him. I recall his satisfaction when we received a cable from Hugo von Hofmannsthal about the placing of a comma. "How we resemble one another!" he said. When a small, last-minute alteration in an essay of W. B. Yeats came as the magazine, already off the press, was about to be sent out to the newsstands, the whole issue was destroyed and a fresh one made.

Like Parliament after some public scandal, the staff held post mortem meetings each month following the publication of the magazine. Scofield would arrive with a long sheet of paper on which he had meticulously noted down every error, and each would be remorselessly tracked to the guilty person. These were painful occasions, redeemed by the presence of Dr. Watson, whose quick and indulgent understanding offered balm to all. The most tangled problem he could unravel, the most ruffled feelings appease. Of course, there is no more unhappy experience for an editor, or for an author, than to have errors he is responsible for jump up at him out of the page like so many stinging scorpions. There are writers who take no pleasure in seeing their work in print because of some mistake in grammar, some redundancy, pleonasm, cliché, or wretched split infinitive (though these are now in fashion) – disgraces, it would seem, almost as great as snatching a purse from an old blind man. But "excel and you will live," and even philosophers have to wrestle with this insidious bribe, as we discover from the following reflection of Seneca's: "Will you not give up striving to keep posterity silent about you? You were born for death. And so to pass the time, write something in simple style, for your own sake, not for publication; they that study for the day have less need of fear."

Who indeed should concern himself with what takes place when death has cast him utterly down? "After fame is oblivion," and one moment of present bliss is worth a millennium of homage to the hieroglyphs of a vanished name. For those of us, however, who have drunk, as from a living fountain, draughts of new, strong life from the written word, who honor certain countries, certain cities, certain villages because we associate them with the names of the authors we have loved, we do not regret a less austere conclusion. "I consider it," writes Montaigne, "to be a great consolation for the frailty and brevity of this life to reflect that there is the power of prolonging it by reputation and renown; and I embrace very readily such pleasant and favourable notions innate in our being, without inquiring too curiously either the how or the why."

Into what delightful paths had my days at last carried me! Surrounded by sympathetic people, subjected to the dilemmas incident only upon making nice aesthetical judgments, with young men and old paying me artful compliments, in touch with minds original and imaginative – the pick of all Europe and America – what higher fortune could I desire? "Fortune turns round like a mill wheel and he that was at the top lies today at the bottom." To find strength and inspiration in the fruits of our own minds is our only firm stake against disaster.

Since my marriage many years have passed, and truth – all things seen under the form of eternity – is still my quarry. Descartes held the belief that everyone should at least once in his life question every social custom, law, and moral code, and he might have added every philosophical and religious conception. To conserve the liberty and singularity of our intellects, the freshness of our poetic vision, amidst so many "turning pictures" and false valuations is an undertaking most delicate. Truth is everywhere and it is nowhere – "it pleases me to doubt not less than to know." All is peculiar, all is magical. We look into a rose and discover a universe, we contemplate a toad and come upon a miracle. Every grass blade is a cry to heaven, every dust mote a whirling planet. To reduce truth to the rational and the logical is to deny truth. "To what men meet each day, men still keep strange."

> For double the image my eyes do see,
> And a double vision is always with me.

Truth is a curlew that gives its clear call; the light flashes, a feather drops at our feet, and it has flown away.

THE END